# Peter W

## Canada's Youngest Serial Killer

**CRIMES CANADA:**

**True Crimes That Shocked The Nation**

*~ Volume 11 ~*

**by Dr. Mark Bourrie**

2

# Peter Woodcock

## Canada's Youngest Serial Killer

**CRIMES CANADA:**

**True Crimes That Shocked The Nation**

*~ Volume 11 ~*

**by Dr. Mark Bourrie**

***www.CrimesCanada.com***

ISBN-13: 978-1523256990
ISBN-10: 1523256990

Copyright and Published (2016)

***VP Publications an imprint of***

***RJ Parker Publishing, Inc.***

*Published in Canada*

## Copyrights

This book is licensed for your personal enjoyment only. All rights reserved. No part of this publication can be reproduced or transmitted in any form or by any means without prior written authorization from Peter Vronsky or RJ Parker of VP Publications and ***RJ Parker Publishing, Inc***. The unauthorized reproduction or distribution of a copyrighted work is illegal. Criminal copyright infringement, including infringement without monetary gain, is investigated by the FBI and is punishable by fines and federal imprisonment.

## Kindle Unlimited

Enjoy these top rated true crime eBooks from VP Publications **FREE** as part of your Kindle Unlimited subscription. You can read it on your Kindle Fire, on a computer via Kindle Cloud Reader or on any smartphone with the free Kindle reading app.

**OR**

Click 'Buy' and own your copy.

**View All Books by RJ Parker Publishing at the following Amazon Links:**

*Amazon Kindle - USA*

*Amazon Kindle - Canada*

*Amazon Kindle - UK*

*Amazon Kindle - Australia*

**View Crimes Canada Book at:**

*rjpp.ca/CC-CRIMES-CANADA-BOOKS*

For Gary Morris, Wayne Mallette, Carole Voyce, Dennis Kerr and their families.

## A Note About Names

The subject of this book has lived with a number of names. I have chosen to call him Peter Woodcock, his birth name, in the early years of his life, although he was also known under his adoptive name of Peter Maynard. In this book, he's called David Michael Krueger from the time that he legally changes his name. David Michael Krueger. Peter Maynard and Peter Woodcock are very much the same person.

# Table of Contents

TORONTO IS A SINFUL PLACE.....................................9
THE MAKING OF A TEENAGE SERIAL KILLER..........35
PHOTOS.................................................................64
THE TRAGEDY.......................................................75
STATEMENT TO POLICE.........................................87
PLAN X.................................................................95
KNIGHT OF THE PRAETORIAN GUARD.................107
INITIATION DAY...................................................123
THE LAST ACT.....................................................137
About Crimes Canada............................................139
Books in the Crimes Canada Collection...............142
ABOUT THE AUTHOR...........................................144
CONTACT INFORMATION.....................................147

8

## TORONTO IS A SINFUL PLACE

Seeley's Bay is a hamlet on the Rideau Canal, 150 miles east of Toronto. The flow of life is connected to the seasons. In the winter, the community is somewhat isolated from the rest of the world. In the summer, pleasure boaters using the Rideau system bring the place to life. With its woodlands and lakes, Seeley's Bay is a great place for a boy to grow up. And it would be Irene Mallette's life-long regret that she didn't keep her son Wayne in Seeley's Bay in the late summer of 1956, instead of taking him to Toronto to visit her mother.

The Mallettes – Irene, her husband John, who was about to turn 50, and their sons, Wayne, a playful seven-year-old, Ronnie, 11, Graham, 17, and John, 21, crammed into the family car on Saturday, September 15, 1956 for a quick trip to Toronto in the family's new car. Back then, before the main expressways in Ontario were built, it took more than four hours to get from Seeley's Bay to Toronto. The big city was nothing like the sprawling metropolis of more than 5,000,000 people that it is today, but it was still, by far, the largest town in Ontario. The skyline was dominated by the Bank of Commerce building, a Manhattan-style skyscraper that soared 34 stories into the air and was the tallest building in the British Empire. To people who lived in the country, Toronto – even when it was a God-fearing, conservative community where every business was closed on Sundays and people in more sophisticated places called it "Toronto the Good" - could be a frightening place. Irene Mallette was anxious as the cramped car went through town after town along the highways to Toronto. "Toronto is a sinful place," she told herself.

Wayne Mallette was a blonde, brown-eyed Grade 1 student. His mother described him as delicate. Wayne was likely premature, and his health problems kept him in a Kingston hospital for the first five months of his life. Still, he was active and he liked to play outside.

The family planned to stay at Wayne's grandmother's home on Empress Street, near the Canadian National Exhibition grounds. That entire neighborhood is gone, replaced by the Gardiner Expressway and its ramps. In 1956, it was part of southern Parkdale, on the western edge of old Toronto. In late August, the neighborhood was busy with people going back and forth to the Exhibition, but in the fall it was quiet. When the Mallettes arrived in the city, the Exhibition's roads were empty, except for popcorn boxes and candy wrappers tossed by the winds. A few guards patrolled the fairgrounds, watching for kids who might try to break into the vacant buildings or climb the idle wooden Flier roller coaster.

Almost as soon as the Mallettes parked the car, the boys took off in separate directions to play. After supper, the older ones went to a movie. The youngest boy pleaded to be allowed to go with his brothers. "Take me to the movie with you," he begged. "Please, please!" But the older boys wanted to stay for the second show and told Wayne they would be out too late for his bed time. Instead, Wayne wandered the grounds of the Canadian National Exhibition, which was shut for the season but, with its ornate old buildings and its empty midway, was still fascinating to a boy from the country.

But the big attraction was the railway line that ran near the neighborhood.

"How he played!," his mother said. "He loved those trains that just roared by."

A half-hour after Wayne left, Irene knew something was terribly wrong.

"I sat at that window and looked for him. I knew, I just knew, that something was wrong. It was as if a voice was telling me 'Wayne's not coming back'."

Jack Mallette, the father, went outside and called for the boy. There was no answer. "No, he's not around," John said. Irene's mother Hazel Armstrong called the police. It was 8:15 in the evening. The sun had gone down and, for the Mallette family, a night of horror began.

When the older boys arrived back from the movies two hours after the police were called, Wayne was not with them. Irene was now convinced something was horribly wrong. The police still hadn't arrived, so Irene called them again, and this time they showed up. Two squad cars came to the door. The police took down a description of the boy, then decided to take John with them as they patrolled the neighborhood.

Soon afterwards, a reporter from the Toronto Star arrived at Hazel Armstrong's house. Irene Mallette was angry and wanted everyone to know it.

"I never liked Toronto. Mothers here just don't know the things that can happen to their children. They have no idea. Happy, cheerful little Wayne didn't know. He had been told about strangers. But what does that really mean to a seven-year-old? Somebody killed Wayne. Somebody killed him and carried him off. I hate this city. But my husband, my sons and I are staying here until we get the person who did this to Wayne. We're not leaving until we get him.

"I pray God will forgive him. We can't."

\*\*\*

The boy had wandered from his grandmother's yard to the main railway line that still runs through the Exhibition neighborhood. The fence along the track was hidden from the nearby houses by trees, but a path ran right along the inside edge of the chain link. It was a perfect place for boys to hide.

Somewhere near the bushes, Wayne met his killer, a teenager with a beautiful new bike. Wayne told the older boy that he had come to watch the trains. It seemed both of them were railway fans. The boys began talking about the freights and passenger trains that were roaring by on the busy tracks. Then the conversation became more dreadful.

The killer took Wayne to a hidden place just west of the Dufferin Gates where, he told the boy, they could see the trains close-up. Then he tried to get Wayne to play "sex games". The killer had molested dozens of other children over the previous summer and usually had no problem conning them into taking off their clothes. Wayne was different. He became scared and wanted to run away. The teenager stopped being friendly. He shoved Wayne's face into the dirt. He kicked the little boy, punched him, bit him viciously on the legs, and shoved trash in his mouth. The killer knew Wayne was dead when he heard his death rattle.

When Constables Smith and Brown found Wayne's body just after midnight, he was lying on his back and there were still tears on his cheeks.

They called the city coroner, Dr. Morton Shulman, who examined the boy's body and was sure he was deliberately smothered. Wayne's body was taken to a forensics lab, where, at 4:45 in the morning, Wayne's father identified it. Dr. Ward Smith examined Wayne, looking for signs that Wayne had not died in an accident or had suffered from a medical condition. Detective Adolphus Payne of the City of Toronto police force, the lead investigator on the case, stayed at the lab while Dr. Smith did his work. It was obvious to Dr. Smith that Wayne Mallette had been murdered. There were few obvious signs of violence, Wayne was fully-clothed and Dr. Smith found no evidence of sexual assault.

During the first day of their investigation, the police thought the killer might be a "sex deviate", one of the flashers who had recently been frightened out of High Park during a recent police crackdown. They searched the houses that had been vacated to make way for the new expressway. There were false leads, but a few strong ones that police, at first, couldn't believe: sightings of Mallette with a youth who was not much bigger than the murdered child, a skinny kid on a flashy bike.

Behind the Exhibition's Food Building, a watchman had stopped to talk to a strange-looking youth, a runtish teenager wearing a grey windbreaker who seemed abnormally friendly. He wanted to know if the guard patrolled the bushes along the railway tracks. The guard said that was the job of the city police. The boy asked him, "Do they ever find any bodies in the bushes? What would you do if you found a body in the bushes?"

"I would call the city police," the guard answered.

"Aren't you a policeman?" the killer asked.

"No," the guard answered. The guard asked the teen if he had seen a body.

"No, but I saw a boy run out of the bushes. He looked just like me."

Then the boy got on his bicycle and rode away.

The guard made a mental note of the strange boy: About 14-16 years old, slight build, just over 5 feet, straight dark hair parted to the side and combed over, grey windbreaker, t-shirt that was white with red horizontal stripes, dark pants or blue jeans, well-spoken with a voice that still seemed boyish, with a very nice touring bike.

"An important clue in the case could be held by a boy about fifteen years of age who was seen riding his bicycle at a fast rate out of the CNE grounds by the Princes' Gate. Police think he may have been riding at a full clip because he had seen something that frightened him," the *Toronto Star* reported.

Detective Payne hoped they could get the teenager to come forward. He issued a statement to the press saying the youth was not wanted as a suspect, just as a witness who might be able to give the police information that might help them find the killer. They didn't say they had found bike tracks leading from the murder scene. They weren't clear enough to make plaster casts, but they definitely showed someone had left on a bicycle. "There is little doubt the youth (the guard) was talking to is our boy," Detective Payne wrote in a memo the night of the murder.

"This youth mentioned that he came from Weston, and said, 'There's a coffee waiting for me' and 'I have to go up north of Toronto now (or to North Toronto)'."

Police interviewed all of the kids in the neighborhood. They found a couple of girls who had come across a strange boy on a bicycle several times that summer. Usually, he just stared at them, but he had made lewd suggestions to them. The boy, they said, lived on Maynard Avenue, a small street northwest of the crime scene.

After a full night and day of working on the case, investigators Payne and Bernard Simmons went back to the Empress Street house and told the Mallettes that the coroner's investigation was finished and they could start planning Wayne's funeral. The officers then split up, some to talk to juvenile court judges about suspicious boys, some to track down and interview every teenage boy in the neighborhood. Police talked to the parents of every boy, checked alibis, interviewed theatre owners, combed the public washrooms near the crime scenes for clues.

They even came up with another victim. A three-and-a-half-year-old boy named Dennis had been put outside to play on the afternoon of Friday, September 7. The little boy had been allowed to wander into the construction site of the new Gardiner Expressway. His mother could see the boy playing on piles of sand that were left around the construction site. But after about 20 minutes, the child disappeared. His mother started looking for him, but she didn't call the police. Two hours later, a teenage boy dropped Dennis off, telling the child's mother that he had found Dennis wandering around High Park.

According to a police report made after Wayne Mallette's murder, Dennis's mother "noticed that her son looked dazed and on examining him she found that he had a large bump on the back of his head with fresh abrasions, red areas on both sides of the front of his neck with scratch marks between the reddened areas. On his stomach just above his navel were teeth marks.

"On she and her husband questioning Dennis she found that a boy had come along to Dennis while he was playing and had walked him along the new roadway to some bushes (apparently in High Park) where he tied his hands behind his back with some rope or string; had tied some string around his neck; had punched him on the back." The attacker had shown Dennis his penis. The young man who had found Dennis and brought him home was not the assailant. The person who hit Dennis and bit him was younger and smaller, about the same size as his cousin, who was about five feet tall. Dennis's mother took the boy to a nearby hospital on the day of the attack. The doctor had made notes of the boy's injuries, but detectives did not come across the case until they started investigating Wayne Mallette's murder.

They also found adolescent girls in the neighborhood played a very strange game. Boys and girls knew how to make each other cough, gag and even pass out by inserting their fingers into the "V" of the neck and pressing against the windpipe. Firefighters were called to a school the week after Labour Day to rescue a fourteen-year-old girl who could not be revived by her friends. When the police questioned the teens, they said they'd learned about the hold from a boy who was a stranger in the neighborhood.

From the start, police knew the killer was a teenage boy. The morning after the murder, police officers went to every high school in the city with a description of the small, round-faced boy and the lovely bike. They also started checking on boys in the Parkdale neighborhood. They seemed convinced the killer was from that neighborhood, even though the suspicious teenager said he was from the northern part of the city. Experts did forensic tests on Mallette's body and were even able to make a cast of the teeth imprints on the boy's legs. With the eyewitness evidence they had, police believed they had a pretty good chance of solving the case. A $2,000 reward, offered five days after the killing, was also expected to help.

\*\*\*

A few days before Wayne Mallette's murder, fourteen-year-old Ron Moffatt skipped school. That's a normal part of adolescence. So is fear of punishment. Before his parents came home, Moffatt took a blanket and a pillow, went into a crawl space in his family's apartment building basement and hid, sneaking out once in a while to go to a movie. He lived in the cubby hole for four days, long enough that his parents became worried and called the police. The men investigating Wayne Mallette's death seemed so sure it was a boy from the neighborhood, and Moffatt lived very close to the home on Empress Avenue where the angry, tearful Mallette family were still staying, waiting for answers.

Ron Moffatt, like the other boys in the neighborhood, used the exhibition site as their playground. He'd even got a job on one of the rides, The Rotor, during the Exhibition. The show was over at Labour Day, when Moffatt had to go back to school. That hadn't worked out well, and now Moffatt was in trouble for skipping school.

The night of the murder, Moffatt had gone to a movie, then snuck back into the basement. The main features playing at the Metro Theatre, *Ulysses* and *Last Hunt*, ran from 5:30 to 9:30 p.m. These times would turn out to be very important.

After Wayne Mallette's body was found, police began to seriously search for the Moffatt boy. Detectives Payne and Simmons began a search of Moffatt's apartment building. At 12:20 p.m. on Friday, September 21, they searched the basement and found the cubby hole. Moffatt was curled up under a blanket, asleep. The officers loaded Moffatt into the back of a squad car, where the boy sat hunched on the seat, his face buried in his hands. The police asked him why he had been hiding. "I couldn't stand it anymore, I had to do something or say something about a fight that occurred in the house and my mother and father throwing water at each other."

Detective Payne corrected him. "It's what happened at the Exhibition Grounds that we are talking about? Were you down at the Ex?"

Moffatt answered "Yes."

They went straight to police headquarters in downtown Toronto. The officers asked the boy when he'd last been at school. Moffatt, it turned out, had been skipping school since the previous Monday. He said he was good at art. He'd had a few odd jobs, washing cars, being a pin boy at a bowling alley, working on a ride at the Exhibition.

They talked about the night of Mallette's murder. The investigators became convinced they had the right young man.

"Just a minute, Ron," Payne said. "The way this thing is going now, it's only fair to let you know that you are going to be charged with murder."

Moffatt began to say something. Payne stopped him, then read a pre-printed caution about his rights. Moffatt began to talk very quickly, and Simmons began writing it all down.

The detectives molded the boy into the murder suspect they were looking for. They even played out their scenario on the front page of the *Toronto Star*:

"Police have learned that the boy and Wayne became locked in a struggle in the bushes, the latter getting a grip on the older boy. The suspect is reported to have bitten him twice to loosen Wayne's hold, then grabbed him by the neck and held him face downward until he died of suffocation.

"He felt the boy's body go limp, knew he was dead and then became frantic.

"He pedaled away on a stolen bicycle after speaking to a CNE guard. It is reported the bicycle was found after the boy's arrest in a spot along the railway tracks near Fort York armouries. He abandoned it after riding it out the gate and north to Strachan Avenue."

It was damning stuff. Of course, the Moffatt's parents denied it and gave an alibi for their son. The police should have listened. Moffatt was five inches taller than the boy who had been seen around the CNE grounds. He wore black loafers, not running shoes. For the last four days, he had been wearing a pink silk shirt, not a white t-shirt. His windbreaker was rust-colored, not grey. He did not have a bike.

But, after some prodding, he confessed.

Moffatt said he was planning to hang around the empty exhibition grounds. He wandered around the band-shell and earned a bit of change helping a man unload a truck. He sat around for a bit, then a boy came up to him and started teasing.

"I told him to go away and he wouldn't pay attention to me, he kicked me, I got up and started to fight with him, I got my arm on his neck and I put too much pressure on, I got up and I spoke to him and he didn't answer. I was scared so I moved his body, then I took the bike and headed for the Princes' Gate. A watchman seen me near the Pure Food building and I started talking to the watchman and that's when I asked him if he had seen a boy on a bike... ride out from the bushes that looked like my twin or something like that.

"I said what would happen if you found a dead person lying around here, and he said he would contact the police. By that time we were near the Strachan Gate and he pointed the way out and said 'that's the way out' and I left him. I went behind the armouries near the railroad track and that's where I put the bike there, amongst a bunch of small trees... I went to Johnny's Restaurant and had something to eat."

The next day, according to the confession, Ron Moffatt went to school. He was worried about the description that was broadcast on the radio.

Moffatt supposedly offered to take the detectives on a tour of the crime scene. Before he left, Moffatt told his mother he had killed Wayne Mallette. "Tell me what happened," she said to Ron, who was sitting in a chair, sobbing. "Did you do it?"

"I did," he answered.

"Do you mean you killed that boy at the Ex?"

"Yes," Ron answered.

"Oh, why did you have to do that?"

"I don't know, we got into a fight," Ron answered.

Then he went to the Exhibition grounds. The detectives drove him to the place where Wayne Mallett's body was found, then showed Moffatt the place where he had talked to the watchman. The police drove Moffatt to the University of Toronto's dental school, where casts were made from his teeth. Detective Payne asked why Moffatt had bit Wayne

Mallette. Making a biting motion, he said, "I just get a feeling. It seems like I like to bite flesh." The officers asked Moffatt if he had bit Dennis, the little boy found in High Park. Moffatt said he wasn't sure. He might remember if he saw a picture of the boy.

At about the same time, a neighbor wrote a note to police, saying he had given the tip that led to Moffatt's capture, and asking for that $2,000 reward.

\*\*\*

"Basically, the police wrote the confession," Moffatt, now a retired school caretaker in Northern Ontario, said in 2015. "They played 'good cop-bad cop' and beat the confession out of me. They filled in anything that I got wrong. Then they took me to the crime scene and showed me around. That was supposed to be part of the confession. The police told the newspapers I showed them the crime scene, which wasn't true." Still, police wrote long, detailed memoranda about the tour of the Exhibition grounds, including the crime scene. Taken on their face value, the documents filed by the police show detailed, damning evidence supposedly given up by Moffatt that seemed to prove his guilt.

There were quite a few other problems with the prime suspect. For one thing, he couldn't ride a bike, and one thread that connected all of the eyewitness accounts of the Mallette disappearance was that the suspect was riding a very nice bicycle.

"I couldn't ride a bike," Moffatt said, almost sixty years after he was arrested. "I was a boxer in high school. I got hit in the ear and I have a bad sense of balance. The cops found a bicycle and said I stole it."

And he had an alibi.

"A friend of mine was an usher in a theatre on Bloor Street. At the time of the murder, I was sitting with his girlfriend. The police said I had time to sneak out, ride a bike down to the Exhibition grounds, commit the murder and get back."

Witness after witness – other movie-watchers, staff at the theatre, friends of Moffatt's, confirmed he was at the theatre.

He'd even stayed behind to help change the letters on the movie sign. The last movie ended at 9:30, more than an hour after the first phone call to the police reporting Mallette missing, and almost certainly well after the watchman and the killer had spoken to each other. It took some time to change the sign letters, so Moffatt was almost certainly at the theatre until well after 10 p.m. The people who had seen Moffatt were all willing to testify at the trial, but nothing they said could trump that confession.

Once they got the "confession," the detectives closed the case and packed Moffatt off to reform school. His trial was held just over a month after the murder, but it was more of a formality than anything. John Mallette, Wayne's father, was left angry and frustrated, and wrote letters to the police demanding the name of Ron's father so he could go after him.

"They used to tell me at the Church Street juvenile detention centre, 'you know, when you're 18, they're going to hang you.'" Moffatt did things that didn't help his own case. In the early months of 1957, he and another teen escaped from the Bowmanville reform school east of Toronto. They were caught and put on a starvation diet. During the day, they had to clean a terrazzo floor with a toothbrush. At night, they slept on the same floor with just one blanket. Soon afterward, Moffatt was sent to the Guelph Reformatory, a tough jail for adults. He was too young to be placed in the general population. Instead, Moffatt was housed in the jail's psychiatric ward, awaiting sentencing.

"I was terrified. I was supposed to be a child killer. I expected to be in serious danger. But the guys in there took me under their wing. They seemed to know that I was not guilty. When I was told that my appeal would be heard by the court, they cheered. The police brought me back to Christie Street. One of the mean old guards said 'You'll never get out.'"

But he did. The real killer, Peter Woodcock, had been caught and was eager to confess to Wayne Mallette's murder. "I went to court the next day and was acquitted. The whole weight of the world was lifted off my shoulders."

Moffatt wonders to this day whether he would have spent decades in jail if Woodcock had not been caught. Although he spent less than a year in custody, Moffatt's youth was ruined.

"After I was acquitted, I ended up at the psychiatric hospital in Toronto, and later on at the psychiatric hospital in Whitby.

"As soon as I was acquitted, the Crown (prosecutor) jumped up and said there would be no compensation. My parents said they wouldn't go to court for it. They couldn't afford it. They had already sold all the furniture to pay the lawyer. They had disconnected their phone because they got so many threatening calls.

"I can understand that. People thought their son was a child killer. Even after I was acquitted, a lot of people thought there had to be more to it, that I was guilty somehow. We all just wanted to put it behind us.

"I was an emotional wreck until I was in my mid-20s. I had to get out of it on my own. I worked, read. I was a history buff. I kept the secret to myself. My first wife eventually told our kids what happened after they grew up. To me, it was 100 years ago. I met a psychiatrist who said he couldn't believe that I was OK. He thought for sure I would live the rest of my life in a psychiatric ward."

Instead, he raised two children, worked all his life, and now draws political cartoons for a local news web site.

## THE MAKING OF A TEENAGE SERIAL KILLER

The real killer read all about Moffatt's arrest with considerable interest, and some anger, too. He didn't want someone else taking "credit" for one of his crimes. There were so many clues in the Mallette murder that pointed to him. Even the front page headline in the *Toronto Star*, "Boy Murdered in CNE Grounds Seized While Watching Trains" should have set off a few alarm bells in the killer's adoptive family, who were so well aware of the teenager's railway and streetcar fetish.

It's not clear why Ron Moffatt confessed to the murder of Wayne Mallette. Probably, as he says, he was forced to do it. The police officers who investigated this case some six decades ago are long gone, so they can't defend themselves. The written record they left behind is either an intricate and very believable series of false confessions or a collection of police reports that were very carefully crafted to frame Moffatt.

The real seeds of Wayne Mallette's murder were sown in the months before the beginning of World War II. On March 5, 1939, in a ward of a Toronto hospital, a strange, fussing baby was born out of wedlock. It didn't stay with its mother for long: Children's Aid social workers were beginning the task of disposing of it. The child was named Peter by his mother Juanita. She was either a seventeen-year-old factory worker or a nineteen-year-old prostitute from eastern Ontario. Either way, she was supposed to have been active and attractive. His father was alleged to be a nineteen-year-old soldier, and the records make it appear that World War II brought them together. Again, the written record is misleading. A little math shows Juanita Woodcock got pregnant in 1938, many months before Canada began mobilizing for the war.

Four years later, she gave birth to another baby, a girl, who was adopted and, according to a report by social workers, led a normal life. Until at least the 1990s, she never found her long-lost brother, if she'd looked for him at all.

Juanita breastfed Peter for a month, then scooped him up and put him in a foster home. He screamed constantly and he wouldn't eat. The baby's crying never stopped, so the Children's Aid moved him from one set of foster parents to another. He never slept, he never ate, and no one could stand to be near him. The Children's Aid's social workers were used to moving babies from home to home. At the time, it was the agency's policy to frequently switch foster homes because they didn't want the temporary "mothers" to get too attached to the babies. The troubling, unnerving behavior lasted all of that first year. The various foster parents tried different diets to try to get the baby to gain weight, but nothing worked and he became more bizarre.

As a toddler, he was terrified of anyone who came near him. He learned to talk when he was approaching two years, but the speech was incoherent. It wasn't ordinary baby talk. People described it as a series of strange whining noises. He was an odd baby growing up in homes of people who didn't want him. Some of the foster families were uncaring, cold and brutal. Since the foster families weren't allowed to adopt him or even get to know him well, they basically kept their distance and looked after Peter for the money that Children's Aid paid them. Once, the weird baby was brought into a hospital emergency ward with a twisted neck, the result of a beating by one of the foster parents. His clinical file is much too silent about this period in his life, but Krueger's memory of years of neglect and abuse is credible:

"When I was put up for adoption, I was bounced around from place to place. I was ignored for long periods of time, left to lie in darkness. Hardly anyone ever picked me up, held me or things like that. This happened in foster homes and other institutions. There was no attempt at bonding," he says. Finally, when he was three years old, he was sent to his last foster home. Frank and Susan Maynard were an upper-middle-class couple with a son of their own who lived in one of the better sections of what was then northern Toronto, the Yonge Street-Lawrence Avenue area. Throughout the war, the Maynards had taken in orphaned and poor children until permanent homes were found for them. Why they ended up hanging on to Woodcock is a mystery. Likely, they just felt sorry for him. There was room in the Maynards' spacious home for one more child. The house is gone now and a church stands on the site, but pictures of the place show that it was one of those ample, three-story Edwardian homes built on a shady, quiet street. Frank Maynard was an accountant who seems to have fit well with the image of the stereotypical father of the 1940s and 1950s. His son, George, was ten years older than the little boy who had come to live with him. George and Peter were never very close. George saw Peter as just one of a string of kids passing through, and by the time the Maynards decided to keep Peter, George was a teenager. When the killings started, George was a university student. He went on to become a successful lawyer.

In some ways, Peter settled into the household quickly, growing very conscious of his new middle-class standing. In fact, a sense of class snobbery developed faster than most of his other social instincts. He looked down on the poorer people of Toronto, families like the ones he had stayed with in his earlier foster homes. This class consciousness would play out in Woodcock's crime patterns. There's no record of Woodcock harming kids in wealthier neighborhoods of the city. He always committed his crimes in the poorer parts of town.

Most of his views on class seem to have come from his new foster mother, Susan Maynard. She was a plump, short woman from a wealthy Maryland background. Susan comes across as a tyrant in most conversations with Krueger, and there's no doubt that she was forceful, with an overly-developed sense of what was proper. Still, she must have had a tremendous amount of charity, strength and patience to deal with the baby that she had taken into her home. In all of the records kept on the family, there was never a suggestion that she wanted to give her weird child back, and she had many chances. She also had many reasons. Peter still screamed any time a stranger approached and he looked like a child with rickets. For Susan, raising Peter was a full-time job. She became attached to Peter and defensive, insisting to skeptical doctors and friends that her damaged little toddler was improving.

"I have several earliest memories," Krueger says. "One is being carried by my foster mother, backwards and forwards across the living room. I was around three years of age. The radio was playing. Probably it was classical music. It was in music that I defined my emotions as a child because it could be joyous or sad."

Next door, Frank Maynard built a skating rink for the two boys on a vacant lot.

Peter wished they had stayed in that house, but when he was ten, they moved to Lytton Boulevard, to the place which later became notorious as the home of Peter Woodcock, child killer. It was a spacious house, with a large sunroom and an attached garage. The Maynards and their foster son settled into a comfortable, substantial home with antique gaslights that still worked.

\*\*\*

Gradually, people began agreeing with Susan that Peter seemed to be getting better, at least physically. He had stopped screaming around strangers. At the same time, by the age of seven, he was already developing the pool of knowledge that he draws on for his fantasy world. He had a sharp memory for details and developed a strong vocabulary. Learning things gave him something to do to fill his time. He was usually alone: other kids thought he was strange and wouldn't play with him. Being small, weak, strange and homely, he was a natural target for bullies. Throughout his life, he would always be an outsider and vulnerable to physically stronger people, and his fear and resentment would be the fuel that fed his cruel inner world.

For five years, starting at the age of seven, Woodcock was treated for his behavior problems by doctors at the Hospital for Sick Children. The entire family needed help coping. The Maynards were well into middle age and the strain of looking after this strange boy was causing trouble in their home. Peter's problems had overwhelmed the family and taken over Susan Maynard's life. She stopped being centered on her own son and her husband and now focused all of her time and strength on her damaged foster son. Her time was organized around their frequent trips to the hospital.

When they weren't downtown seeing specialists, the mother and boy were home at their comfortable house, with its overstuffed furniture, its knickknacks and mementos. On a mantel, there was a set of Indian War-vintage army knives Susan brought with her from her childhood home. Krueger remembers the snow falling outside the house's bay windows, the blinking Christmas lights, Susan coming in to light the gaslight in his room. She warned him never to turn the gaslight off, only down, so that gas fumes couldn't leak. There was a little electric light over his bed so he could read, and Krueger used it every night.

During the day, the boy indulged his urge to wander the city and he developed a fetish for public transportation. "Toronto back in the forties and fifties was an exciting place to grow up," he said one winter day in Penetanguishene, when the roads to the isolated institution deep in the Ontario snow-belt were barely passable. "I went to the Santa Claus Parade in 1946 or 1947 and watched it go down University Avenue. When it was over, we walked to Yonge Street, where there was an even more fantastic parade: all these streetcars, which had been made to wait at the intersections until the parade was over. I was fascinated. They were so exotic. I spent about an hour on Yonge Street with Mother and watched all the streetcars on the side streets until they vanished, and there were just the Yonge cars running up and down.

"Everything seemed bigger, those red and green streetcars on their tracks, one right after the other, all filled with people. I used to sneak on them, and the drivers soon got to know me. I would go all the way down to Queen, then take another streetcar that looked similar but a little different, and head on out to see where it went. When it got to the end of its line, I would take another streetcar. One time I got lost, at the age of four, and ended up in Port Credit, watching the Credit River flow by. Just to the north were empty fields. So I invested a nickel and called home. It was then I had my first encounter with the police, a couple of nice, friendly men dressed in blue."

The Maynards took these travels seriously and tried to get the staff at the Hospital for Sick Children to do something about the boy's wandering. And all of his trips away from home were not nearly so romantic or carefree. Several nights, he never came home, and one time his parents searched all evening and found him hiding in the neighborhood, cowering under bushes. He said he was hiding from other children and that he wanted to stay out where God could protect him.

Strange things began happening inside the house, too.

One day, Susan left the house for twenty minutes and came back to find her canary dead. Peter had laid it out on the piano, surrounded by candles. He told his mother that the family dog had killed the bird. She was mortified by the murder of the canary and scared that Peter would burn the house down. Other times when he was left alone, he tore down the window blinds, chopped up all of his socks, carved symbols into the dining room table and smashed a radio. He liked to sit alone and cut his clothing.

Of course, to David Michael Krueger, the strange behavior was someone else's fault:

"After I was six, seven or eight, Mother hit me with a beaded rod. Mother underwent a marked change in her personality. Something mysteriously happened. They were in New York, and my brother, who was ten years older than me and so was a teenager, was looking after me. He was out with his friends and had left me alone. I went all across the city, going on all of the streetcar routes. When Mother came home, she was brought into the house on a stretcher. In whispers, they told me Mother was pushed down the stairs in Grand Central Station by a drunk who tried to get her purse. She came home with a concussion. We had to be very quiet, very considerate.

"She was allowed to do whatever she wanted, yell, scream or cry at us, but we were not allowed to answer back. My brother started doing the normal teenage thing, staying out. Then the beatings started for me.

"There were good times, too. I remember on my ninth birthday, she took me aside at the celebration and said 'You're nine years of age. When you're outside, you represent the family. When people see you, they will judge the rest of us by how you behave. So be on your best behavior. Remember, we trust you'."

That last story doesn't fit with the psychiatric record. In fact, anything good that he says about his childhood should be taken with a healthy ration of cynicism. Nothing in his files suggests he was anything but a weird little kid looking at the world through pop-bottle-bottom glasses.

Whether or not he was a trusted ambassador of the affluent Maynard family, Woodcock was on the move. He started tracing all the streetcar lines on maps that he kept in his bedroom, exploring neighborhoods, climbing through ravines. There was only one place he wouldn't go: Regent Park, which was then the toughest part of Toronto.

\*\*\*

When he wasn't physically wandering around the city, he was travelling mentally. At school, he chewed pencils and stared out the window. He created fantasy worlds where he was the all-powerful leader.

"It was safer being by myself. I got picked on because I was smaller, uncoordinated. I used to walk crab-like. Even as a teenager, in the Sea Cadets, I would find myself walking with my right arm and right leg coming out together."

Lots of bright, awkward kids are picked on and labeled nerds by their school mates. Very few of them become killers. Woodcock did not kill by lashing out at his tormentors. Instead, he found much younger, weaker, poorer children.

The Maynards and the Children's Aid Society knew Peter had problems. They tried to shelter him from other kids, but the only thing that could have worked would have been a decision to pull him out of school and teach him at home or have him institutionalized with other damaged children. Instead, the Maynards decided to give him the benefits of a private school education.

The first one was near the Maynard home. Waycroft School had a very small student body, but it didn't matter. Any group of children was likely to cause Peter trouble. He wouldn't play games or try to make friends. Sometimes, he came home very disturbed, and he had a couple of bouts of twitching that each lasted two weeks. It was obvious he needed more help than any regular school could give.

As Woodcock became more strange, his foster mother became more protective.

One day, as she sat in a small, grim office at the Hospital for Sick Children, she turned to Dr. Hawke, a psychologist, and said, "I think Peter would do better if we legally adopted him."

Hawke looked at her, turning a greenish shade of white, and said, "For God's sake, woman, don't do that. You don't know what the future holds."

Susan Maynard did give up on the idea of adopting Peter, but she kept looking for a place that could help him. Even though he was still a ward of the Children's Aid, she was willing to pay for the best institutions. The better ones, in the United States, were full, so she tried the schools for disturbed children in Toronto, looking for one that she thought could help Peter.

"One place should have been called Stalag II. It was run by two British ex-Marines who had undergone a sex change," Krueger says. The other schools seemed no better, so Susan began travelling the province to find a place in the country that could help her boy.

In 1950, when Woodcock was eleven and Susan was busy with her search, Peter was sized up by a Children's Aid Society social worker. He was being considered for a school for disturbed children in Kingston, Ontario. Children's Aid enshrined this description in its records:

"Slight in build, neat in appearance, eyes bright, and wide open, worried facial expression, sometimes screwing up of eyes, walks brisk and erect, moves rapidly, darts ahead, interested and questioning constantly in conversation. Peter's main interests appear to be walking his dog, riding his bicycle and attending the Salvation Army meetings. At the Exhibition, he wanted most to see the Canadian Armed Services in Action - the show's planes, tanks and anti-aircraft equipment. He attributes his wandering to feeling so nervous that he just has to get away. In some ways, Peter has little capacity for self-control. He appears to act out almost everything he thinks and demonstrates excessive affection for his foster mother. Although he verbalizes his resentment for other children, he has never been known to physically attack another child. He becomes angry with adults, especially when he feels misunderstood. He seems to handle his fears by avoiding — for example, staying inside when there are other children on the street...

"He kisses the mother two or three times on each departure ...

"Peter apparently has no friends. He plays occasionally with younger children, managing the play. When with children his own age, he is boastful and expresses determinedly ideas which are unacceptable and misunderstood. Recently, Peter was to be included in a Club on the street to raise money for the Red Cross. He wanted to have a Dog and Cat Club and when turned down, he told the boys he liked animals a lot better than boys, thereby immediately losing his place in the club."

The boy, only eleven years old, was already sending out danger signals. When a Children's Aid social worker who was helping with the assessment walked with him through the crowded Canadian National Exhibition grounds on an August day, Peter turned to him and said, "I wish a bomb would fall on the Exhibition and kill all the children."

\*\*\*

Eventually, the Maynards and the social workers settled on a solution. The Children's Aid Society sent him to Sunnyside Children's Centre in Kingston. The fearful, thin but somewhat friendly child fit into the routine of this special school for disturbed children, the same way he fit in with the inmates of the hospital for the criminally insane for so many years. He preferred reading to any kind of physical activity. When adults weren't around, he played sexual games with the other kids. At summer camp in 1952, he spent his time in the wilderness walking around with armloads of books. When counselors found him lying on the side of the road, he told them that he just wanted to see how the underside of cars looked. On quiet days, he sat on a curb with a watch and a Kingston bus schedule, making sure the transit system was running efficiently.

The Kingston school wanted to discharge him when he was fourteen, which was the normal age for release, but social workers thought he was not ready to be on the loose again in Toronto. He talked too much about The Winchester Heights Gang, an imaginary group of boys that Woodcock led on adventures. In real life, he was caught fondling an eleven-year-old girl.

The years in Sunnyside were the best times of his life, he says. He missed Toronto, but he wasn't picked on by other kids at the Kingston school. The new horn-rimmed glasses that he was fitted out with when he was fourteen made him look even more geeky, but he still fit in much more easily with the Sunnyside kids. The staff trusted him to go on his bicycle, and it was in Kingston that his fetish for transit punctuality reached full bloom. He began collecting schedules and watching to see if the city buses ran on time. Woodcock shared a bedroom in an old mansion with three other children.

Despite the progress that Woodcock had made, nearly everyone involved knew that returning Woodcock to the Maynard home in

September 1954 was a mistake. He was sent back to Waycroft, the private school, where he tried to fit in by joining the glee club and the drama club.

After a year at Waycroft, he went to Lawrence Park Collegiate, where kids who recognized him from public school started picking on him again. Six weeks after the school year began, he wanted out. Some of the students pushed him down an embankment and broke his bike. They ripped the Sea Cadet badges that he had earned in Sunnyside off his jacket. Three days later, he started at Bloordale College School, a small private institution, as a Grade 9 student. He stayed there, miserable, until Grade 11, "when the police mercifully put an end to my education and my career."

A new, wonderful white and red three-speed bicycle, which replaced the one broken by the Lawrence Park students, was evolving into the centerpiece of Peter's fantasy world. He led the "Winchester Heights Gang" of five hundred invisible but obedient boys as he pedaled for miles across Toronto and the farmland north of the city, which, in those days, began close to the Maynard home.

"When I was living at home, especially in my teenage years, I rode my bike everywhere. You can go places on a bicycle that people on foot would need a long time to get into."

And, he said, there were always bigger, tougher, and very real bullies in pursuit, despite the phantom presence of the Winchester Heights Gang.

"I would go tearing down the Humber River, often doing forty miles an hour, with people hollering, 'Hey, kid, you're going to lay her down'. I would ride along the lake, just outside the break-wall all the way through to the Western Gap and come back in on Parliament Street. I would make that trip in half an hour, from Eglinton to the Humber, or sometimes I would just take off up the Don River."

When he wasn't riding, he was stopping adults on the street to ask questions and trying to get to know every streetcar conductor in the city. At home, he watched the Mickey Mouse Club and fantasized that the Winchester Heights gang was doing some of the same things that Mickey's friends did. But he had no friends his own age, only the TV, the radio, and his classical music records. That summer, he got a job parking cars at Casa Loma, a giant mansion that is one of Toronto's busier tourist attractions. No one except Peter knew what he was doing on those long bicycle trips.

\*\*\*

The awful dreams of murder and rape started in February 1956.

At the same time, a new, "alien" self seemed to enter Woodcock's body. That was the way he saw the strong attraction that he was developing for small children and the vicious fantasies he had, day and night, about killing them. Every time he saw a child, he wondered what its private parts looked like. When he led the invisible Winchester Heights Gang, they went on much more evil missions.

Woodcock began acting on his new urges by playing sex games with small children, bribing them with rides on his wonderful bike. At first, there was no violence:

"I was afraid of blood. There were so many people who were willing to come with me that I felt, 'why should I have bothered going on to the next phase'."

"I wanted to go on to the next phase (of criminality) in March of '56. There was a ten-year-old girl. I did have plans to cut her up to see what she looked like inside. And that was the incident, plus the way that it was responded to, that laid the groundwork for the tragedies. We got lost in the ravine in the dark, and getting out seemed more important. I had a pen knife with me. When you're naive, a pen knife seems like enough to kill with.

"It was a turning point. I was already troubled with my fantasies and dreams. This ten-year-old girl, I did have plans of killing her. It didn't dawn on me that she would die. Well, I knew she would die, but that would be about the extent of it. I wanted to look at the arm, see how the muscle attaches to it. This was going to be a very thorough anatomical lesson, though I don't believe I would have been able to name a third of the things I would have seen."

Nothing seemed to go right. The rendezvous was late because Woodcock had dawdled, there was only about an hour of daylight left, and he didn't want to get lost in the ravines in the dark. The stream valleys in central Toronto are a confusing series of steep hills, and this murder failed because Woodcock didn't know them as well as he thought. It took a lot longer than he had expected to get to the place that Woodcock had chosen for the murder. Woodcock and the girl looked for a better scene for the murder, then became afraid of being lost. After wandering around for three hours, they decided to climb out of the ravines and wait for another chance.

The girl's parents had become worried and they talked to the police about Woodcock, but nothing came of the expedition until Woodcock was arrested almost a year later. The police did visit the Maynard house, setting off Woodcock's foster mother. She threatened to ground him for the rest of his life because of the scandal of having a police car parked in front of the house.

"Okay," said Woodcock, "I'll kill myself, if it will make it easier for you to hold your head up with the neighbors. If you don't want me to kill myself, I think I'll just go up to bed because I've got to go to school tomorrow."

He went up to his room. His parents followed and sat on the edge of the bed, where the fight continued. After a few minutes, Mother stormed out of the room. Woodcock's foster father stayed behind.

"Don't pick up any more children," he said quietly.

A couple of months later, after the spring floods ran through the ravines and the new leaves hid the river valleys and kids' play forts, Woodcock started travelling the city on his bike. His attacks became more violent. He would choke children until they passed out, peer over their bodies, then leave them to wake up, alone and naked, in a park or ravine. Many of them never told their parents.

Two weeks after he killed Wayne Mallette, Woodcock was given a Rorschach ink blot test by the Children's Aid Society that showed he had a large amount of cold-blooded hostility. His mother later said he should have seen a psychiatrist, but instead, she protected him, he would say later, "from Society". Woodcock slid in and out of his dream world, kept watch on the streetcars, and supervised the construction of the expressway that was built through the scene of his first murder.

\*\*\*

That fall, while managing to hold a Saturday job at Casa Loma, Woodcock went out every weekend to molest children. He was working up to another killing. The teen was becoming more ferocious than most adult serial killers, barely waiting for the intense publicity of his last homicide to subside before attacking again.

Only three weeks were to pass from the time Wayne Mallette died until Woodcock killed Gary Morris, a nine-year-old boy from an impoverished downtown neighborhood. Again, Woodcock had left his upper-middle class home to kill a child from a poorer part of the city.

Woodcock had picked the scene in advance. It was Cherry Beach, a neglected piece of Toronto shoreline east of the city's docks. Woodcock met Morris at the St. Lawrence Market and talked the boy into going for a ride on what should have been one of the most famous bikes in the city. One of Morris's friends saw him go and later gave a description of Woodcock to the police, but they couldn't solve this murder.

"I believe he lived on Sackville (in Regent Park). I ran into him in the St. Lawrence Market. He was wandering around, and he liked the bike. I was always on the prowl for someone, and since he was so interested in the bicycle, he seemed like a good catch. He was small, only nine years old. I asked if he wanted to go for a ride, and he said 'sure'. He rode on the bar, sidesaddle. I had better control of the bike that way. Cherry Beach was about a mile away. I knew Toronto well, and I had several of these parts picked out."

Woodcock took him to the foot of Commissioners Street, to an empty waterfront area east of the city port. He choked the child into unconsciousness, took off his clothes, looked at the boy's body, then viciously attacked him. Gary Morris's body was found with bite marks on the neck. The boy had been beaten so hard that he died of a ruptured liver.

"It was just like all the other mistakes. This time, he died as a result of my activities. I realized it when I heard the death rattle. I went home late in the afternoon thinking, 'my God, this has got to stop'."

For a couple of days, no one believed Morris had been kidnapped. He had run away from home a couple of times and may have been doing it again when he walked to the St. Lawrence Market. He had wanted to go to the United States to join the circus.

"There was a big stink, like the Exhibition one, but it was prolonged because they didn't find him for a week or ten days," the boy's killer said years later. "The tall grass is what hid him. After that, they cut it down.

"I was very frightened. I didn't want this to happen again. I didn't want them to die like that. People were getting mad. Toronto was very Victorian, but what didn't help was the circulation war that was still going on between the Toronto Star and the Telegram. If there was an accident and someone was killed, the papers would cover it with big headlines. A story about a murder became huge news."

Despite Krueger's lies to the contrary, Morris's death was no accident.

"It is a long time ago, but I still have memories of it. The memories are like a dream to me, and just about as relevant. It's like having the memories of a sixteen-year-old in the mind of a fifty-four-year-old man, but I suppose if I knew what went on in the mind of a fifty-four-year-old grandfather, I would be horrified. But, you know, you can feel what you like after the fact, but that don't change anything."

No one seemed to notice that the crime so closely resembled the murder of Wayne Mallette. By then, Ron Moffatt was close to his trial date and was being bounced from jails to reform school to psychiatric hospitals.

Soon, Woodcock killed again. This time, the police couldn't miss, no matter how inept they were.

\*\*\*

## WARNING

**The following pages have graphic photos.**

## PHOTOS
### IMAGE 1:

*The front page of the Toronto Daily Star on January 22, 1957 shows Peter Woodcock and victim Carole Voyce, 4.*
*At top right, Woodcock (with glasses) leaves court after being found not guilty by reason of insanity.*
*At left are victims Wayne Mallette (top), Carole Voyce (centre) and Gary Morris.*
*(Toronto Star File Photos)*

**IMAGE 2:**

*'X' marks the spot where seven-year-old Wayne Mallette was found under bushes just west of the Dufferin Street Gates into the fairgrounds of the Canadian National Exhibition (CNE) on September 15, 1956*

# IMAGE 3:

*The body of Wayne Mallette as found at the CNE grounds. The victim after being undressed was dressed again by the serial killer, who also defecated near the body before escaping through the fairgrounds.*

## IMAGE 4:

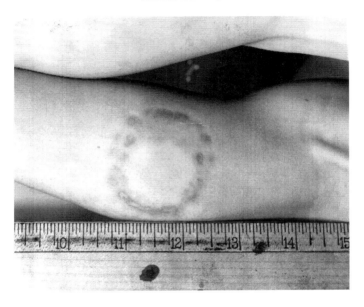

*Evidence photo of the vicious bite left behind by Woodcock on the back of Wayne's leg. Despite the fact that the bite mark would not have matched, another teen suspect was arrested and convicted for the murder while Woodcock went on to kill two more children.*

# IMAGE 5:

*The killing of seven-year-old Wayne Mallette in a relatively crime-free and naive 'Toronto the Good' as it was known at the time, was so brutal and unprecedented that many could not even believe it was a murder, let alone imagine the concept of a "serial killer" in the 1950s. Parents routinely let their kids as young as four years old play and roam around the city streets with little if any supervision.*

## IMAGE 6:

*The body of the second victim, nine-year-old Gary Morris, was found on October 6, 1956 in the opposite side of the city at Cherry Beach. Despite the similarities in the second murder, police were unfamiliar with the concept of a serial homicide and did not make the connection, a phenomenon known as 'linkage blindness." The term "serial killer" itself would not enter into popular usage until 1981.*

# IMAGE 7:

*On January 19, 1957, Woodcock encountered four-year-old Carole Voyce playing in the street near a friends home. He offered her a ride on his bike taking her down into the Don Valley beneath the Bloor Street Viaduct Bridge where he murdered her. Even today, a serial killer's shift from two previous male victims to suddenly a female, would make profilers hesitate before making a link.*

# IMAGE 8:

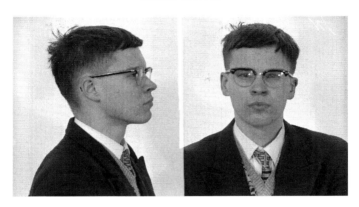

*Portrait of a teenage serial killer. Peter Woodcock mugshot, January 1957. He is seventeen years old.*

# IMAGE 9:

*Peter Woodcock psychiatric facility identity photo in 1959 when Woodcock was nineteen years old.*

**IMAGE 10:**

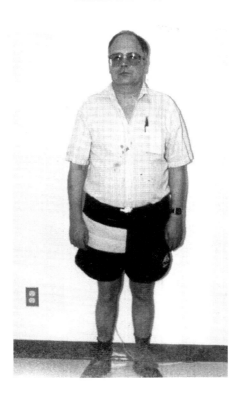

*July 13, 1991: Police photo of Peter Woodcock - - now known as David Michael Krueger--with blood stains on his shirt a few hours after having been issued his first daypass to go into town and buy a pizza after 34 years of confinement and therapy in a criminal psychiatric facility.*

74

## THE TRAGEDY

On Saturday, January 19, 1957, Woodcock got up early and did a few chores around the house. He listened to some music, had lunch, walked to a few stores on Yonge Street, and enjoyed the soft air of a thaw that began to melt the thin layer of snow that had blanketed the city since Christmas.

He went home, wheeled his bike from the porch, and coasted down Yonge Street, past the small stores at Eglinton Avenue, the CHUM building at St. Clair, where disc jockeys were gearing up for the Elvis Presley tour that was starting soon and would bring the King to Maple Leaf Gardens, and down to the Bloor intersection. Woodcock turned left, rode for a while, and stopped at the Danforth Radio Store. Diane Coates, a thirteen-year-old school girl, later told the police that she remembered seeing him in there, and that she had noticed him the summer before in the Jane and Bloor Street areas. There was nothing unusual about Woodcock going into a radio store. In fact, nothing seemed strange that day to anyone who knew him. He was home in time for dinner. After he ate, he went to work at Casa Loma.

At 3:30 that Saturday afternoon, Carole Voyce was playing with her friend Johnny Auld in front of Johnny's apartment house on Danforth Avenue while their mothers visited inside. Johnny's father, William Auld, could also see them from inside the now-defunct Bain Brothers paint store directly below the apartment, where he was working as a clerk. Woodcock rode up to them on that fabulous bicycle. He was wearing a dark windbreaker and blue slacks. His hair was slicked back and he looked at the children through horn-rimmed glasses.

"How old are you?" Woodcock asked the little girl, who had long brown hair, a pretty round face, and who stood only three feet high.

"Four," she replied.

"And how old are you?" he asked Johnny.

"Four," the boy replied.

"How do you like my bicycle?"

"I think it's swell," Johnny said.

"Have you ever been to East York?" Woodcock asked the children.

"No," they answered.

"Have you ever been to the lake?"

This time, the children answered "yes".

"Would you like to go for a ride on my bicycle?"

"Yes," they both said, and the children walked toward the shiny machine and the pimply-faced boy.

"I think I'll take you," he said, pointing at Johnny. Then he paused. "No," he said. "I'll take you," and turned to Carole. "Ladies first."

Then he took her hand and began walking down Danforth Avenue toward the ravines. He balanced the bike with his other hand. Two minutes later, a woman saw Woodcock riding his bicycle along the slushy street, with the girl balanced on the handlebars. She wore a grey snow suit, red mittens and black boots.

Woodcock took the girl to the Don Valley ravine near Auld's house. He talked her into going down the hillside. When she wasn't looking, he had slipped his arm around her neck and choked her until she passed out. Then he jammed his fingers into her eyes. As she choked, she ripped her fingernails on Woodcock's clothes and tore at the mud with her hands. He stripped off her clothes and examined her body, the way he had peered at the bodies of several other unconscious children. Woodcock stuck his fingers in her vagina, then thrust a stick into her body. This was the blow that killed her.

Carole's murderer looked around the ravine and became terrified that he was about to be caught. He tried to push his bike up the steep, wet clay bank, back to the road above. When he slipped back down to the murder scene, he went back to Carole's body and kicked her in the head. Woodcock went into the woods, circled around, and came back to look at the child's body yet again. Then he wheeled his bike to a pathway that led back to the road.

Fred Callum, a railway yard worker, saw Woodcock come up out of the ravine. Other people saw Woodcock, too: a University of Toronto professor who was stopped by the wild-eyed youngster and told: "If there's a murder down there, they'll try to blame it on me." A school mate of Woodcock's saw him ride by. He was hard to miss: few kids rode their bikes in January in the Toronto of the 1950s.

A few minutes after Woodcock took Carole, her mother came out of the Auld apartment and began looking for her.

"Where's Carole?" she asked.

"She's gone for a bike ride with a high school boy," Johnny Auld replied.

The frantic mother called the police, and within ten minutes, two cops, Alex Busby and Earl Snider, arrived at the Aulds' apartment. Ray Voyce got into the car and began cruising the area, while a description of the missing girl was broadcast to police officers across Toronto.

Within ninety minutes of the kidnapping, off-duty officers from nearby police divisions were being called in. A search party was organized shortly after dark. TV stations interrupted their programs to broadcast pictures of Carole and to ask for clues. Sixty police officers searched the area where Woodcock took the girl. Police planned to call in five hundred civil defense volunteers, but they weren't needed. The search for Carole Voyce had ended with the three revolver shots that echoed through the Rosedale ravine, below Toronto's wealthiest neighborhood. Constable Ernie Booth found her frozen and mutilated body near the Bloor Viaduct at 11:09 p.m. His shots signaled the end of a missing person search and the beginning of a manhunt.

Carole's father had searched all evening and was back in a local police station when the police constables at the ravine called in that they had found his daughter's body.

They drove the shattered man to the crime scene, where he had to share the pain that Jack Mallette had endured in the trees by the lakeshore railway tracks. The coroner and forensic experts were averting their eyes and piecing together the crime that had occurred only a few hours before.

For the next three days, police cars patrolled the street in front of Johnny Auld's house in case the killer tried to hurt their best witness. The newspapers ran huge headlines, and on the front page of the Toronto Star was a handwritten note from Raymond Voyce that read:

"To the sick man who did this terrible thing to my little girl. Give yourself up before it happens again."

Toronto Telegram reporter Doug Creighton, in the paper's main front-page story, called Woodcock a "pimply faced sex maniac" and said police were "personally aroused by a murder vicious beyond description."

It was the first big test for the city's new Metro force. More than 2,300 police officers in the Toronto area questioned every teenager who resembled a composite drawing made from the description that Johnny Auld and the other witnesses gave them. Cops who were off-duty were called in to help. Teens were stopped as they walked down the street and were questioned in the park. The day after the murder, one boy tried to run away when police stopped him near the Canadian National

Exhibition grounds. Dozens of cops swept through the area, so close to the scene of Woodcock's first murder. When they caught the teen, they realized he wasn't the murderer. Another boy matching Woodcock's description was grilled for four hours that Sunday afternoon, until police found a witness who saw him in a record store at the time of the murder. Another youth, a Hamilton, Ontario, university student, was arrested on a train because he looked like the boy in the composite drawing.

The drawing was bang on. Yet, the boy the police searched for was already in their office. Woodcock, always a welcome visitor at the station near his house, stopped in to see the police the day after the killing.

"If you're going to do something, the last thing you do is break the patterns that you've set," he told me forty years later, playing the master criminal and, at the same time, underscoring the fact that he was stone crazy by the time he killed Carole Voyce and really had no chance of getting away with that crime.

Already, police had made the connection between Gary Morris's murder at

Cherry Beach and the killing of Carole Voyce. A $5,000 reward was posted. The new Metro Toronto police force finally had its first murder, courtesy of Peter Woodcock, and it had the city on edge.

Constable Jean Newman, a mother of two, went on TV to beg the parents of the murderer to turn in their son and to promise that he would be given a mental examination. On the Monday morning that Woodcock was arrested, his brother, then a law student at Osgoode Hall, sat reading the Telegram in the Maynard family's living room. He looked at the composite, then looked at Peter.

"What have you been doing these days?" he asked jokingly.

"Nothing," said the killer, as he headed out the door to school. Two days after the murder, these were his last hours of freedom.

\*\*\*

He didn't make it through the day. The two police officers who had questioned him after his March trip to the ravine saw the composite, dug through their files, and pulled out Woodcock's dossier. Within an hour, the police were at Woodcock's school.

"It was on my mind every day that I could be caught. I was looking over my shoulder every time that I saw a police cruiser behind me. And my fear was that Mother would find out. Mother was my biggest fear. I didn't know if the police would let her at me.

"After I got caught, I explained it all to her and she was just horrified. She had no idea that she had put me under such pressure. But they did stand by me. If I had been released, I think they would have sent me abroad. Mother was from Maryland, and she knew how they took care of children that had been disgraced. My biggest fear before I was captured was that she would find out first. I knew that whatever she said would be at full decibels, conducted at the highest volume."

The police protected him from "Mother." He escorted them to the place where he killed Carole Voyce, then went back to the police station to be questioned. He babbled on about the other two killings and all

84

of the sexual assaults. Police calmed him down long enough to sign a statement.

86

## STATEMENT TO POLICE
## January 21, 1957

"The first time this happened was in March. You already know the details about that, about the girl. And from then until now I have actually attacked many children, even though I loved children as a rule. I have felt sexually inclined to — I won't go into the number of cases, but will say there must have been about 11 or 12 of them before I met the girl, that is for this case. And I took her for a ride, to the viaduct, as you fellows know about it now, where I subdued her, and I don't know what I did, but she was dead before I realized what I had done and that was about it. Do you want to know from the time I left her and so on? You want to know how I subdued her, I suppose. Well, first of all, I choked her. This is very gruesome, I know. Then I stuck my fingers in her eyes. I don't know why I did that. Isn't it awful?

And then when I tried to clamber up the bank I was frightened by what I did and as I clambered up the little gully there, I slipped and my feet hit her head. Then I left her, circled back on the other side, as you saw my tracks, took one last look and left. And that's all. But it happened so suddenly, I don't know. I can tell you right now that I don't want a trial before a jury. The reason why my parents were not aware of my sickness is because I never told them. I was too ashamed. Do you blame me? I feel relieved now that I have told you the truth because I was worried. Whatever happens, I don't want to go home tonight. I don't want to face my parents.

Signed: Peter Maynard."


"The police treated me with the greatest courtesy. I have nothing (drawing out the word) but the greatest (drawing this word out, too) praise for the police officers who handled my situation and me during the trial. The jail guards teased me about being hanged. That was expected. I knew I was going to hang. As a matter of fact, my lawyer had the greatest difficulty, when the trial opened up, getting me to plead not guilty. Back then, it was a requirement under the law to plead not guilty if you were asking for an insanity verdict. I wanted to go in and say I was guilty of this terrible set of crimes. I wanted to be sentenced to hang. You know, the Diefenbaker government commuted nearly all capital sentences, and I believe, now, that it would have commuted mine. If it had, I would be back on the streets. A commuted capital sentence was twenty years.

"I was in the Don Jail for about nine days, then I went to the Toronto Psychiatric Hospital. I was in jail with a guy named Peter, a hell of a good guy, who had been caught for the same kinds of things I had done. He died here.

"The Don Jail was dismal, but then, it was jail. If you offended, you ended up in jail, and jail was not a Sunday school picnic. The guards would push me down, and sometimes an inmate would make a grab for me through the bars. Even the doctor booted me in the ass several times for what I had done. It sounds terrible, but people thirty-seven years ago would understand it. The Toronto Psychiatric

Hospital was a haven of peace and quiet after that."

The funeral for Carole Voyce was held on the Wednesday after her murder. She wore a new pink dress with long sleeves. Her grandfather, Ernest Voyce, picked out the dress and paid for it.

Meanwhile, prosecutors wrote an indictment for first-degree murder. By then, police, psychiatrists and prosecutors agreed that Peter Woodcock was insane.

"You really don't know your own life until you've been on trial for murder. You learn pretty fast what people think of you. I don't recommend it. When I stood trial, the death penalty was there, on the books, and it was being used. A trial becomes like a game between the Crown and the defence. The judge just sits like a big referee up there," Woodcock said one afternoon over a cheeseburger in the Oak Ridge visitors' center.

About seventy-five people, mostly elderly downtown Toronto residents with a few days of free time on their hands, sat in the old City Hall courtroom and watched Woodcock as he rose in the prisoner's box. The boy, now eighteen, pleaded "not guilty" in a loud, clear voice. Court was adjourned for a few minutes while Woodcock's lawyer, John Brooke, and prosecutor Arthur Klein met in the chambers of Ontario Supreme Court justice W.F. Spence. Likely, the three men put the last touches on an agreement on the outcome of the trial: not guilty by reason of insanity. Back then there was only one fate for murderers acquitted by reason of insanity on a murder charge. Woodcock would be shipped off to Penetanguishene for the rest of his life. First, though, the formalities of the trial had to be carried out.

Once the jury was sworn in, Judge Spence issued a warning:

"May I stress that your sole duty is to bring in a verdict based on the evidence presented here. There was a terrific amount of publicity in this case. Sweep from your mind everything except that which you hear from the witness box. This is a difficult duty for you."

Klein, of course, was unlikely to have problems winning the case, since Woodcock had been a cooperative prisoner who had spent the winter eagerly telling the story of his crimes to anyone who asked about them. The law requires two things to be proven in an insanity defence: that the person on trial committed the crime, and that he did not understand the nature and consequences of his action.

Back then, when a sentence to Penetanguishene was effectively life imprisonment, prosecutors usually agreed to an insanity verdict if one or two respected psychiatrists said the prisoner was unaware of the nature and consequences of his actions because he had a mental disorder. These days, they resist because they worry an insanity verdict is a ticket back to the street.

Many people had come forward to say they had seen him on Bloor Street and around the viaduct that afternoon. The secretary, the railroad watchman, the professor who had been stopped by the crazy young man, the schoolboy who was washing his car had all received subpoenas.

After four days, the trial was over, and the judge wrote out his verdict:

*IN THE SUPREME COURT OF ONTARIO*

*Thursday, the 11th day of April, 1957*

*BETWEEN*

*The Queen and Peter Woodcock*

The Accused, Peter Woodcock, having on the 8th, 9th, 10th and 11th days of April, 1957, been brought before this court sitting with a jury at the City of Toronto in the County of York in the Province of Ontario, charged with murder and a jury empanelled having found that the accused was not guilty on account of insanity

This Court doth order that the accused, Peter Woodcock, be kept in strict custody in Toronto Psychiatric Hospital in the said County of York, until the pleasure of His Honour the Lieutenant Governor of the Province of Ontario shall be known.

Wishart G. Spence, J.

The beautiful cream and red bike, with all of its bells and whistles, was rolled out of the courtroom by a bailiff. It was later given to an orphanage, where, hopefully, its riders never learned its back story.

No one who had been in that courtroom in the spring of 1957 would have guessed that Woodcock would get the chance to kill again. He was destined for what was then called the hospital for the criminally insane in Penetanguishene. The institution, called Oak Ridge, had never released a murderer.

# PLAN X

In time, nearly everything that the jury heard about Woodcock would be glossed over by social workers and psychiatrists, and time would dim the public's memory of his crimes. Time, however, never changed the viciousness in Woodcock or took away his thirst to hurt anyone he could overpower. Time and psychiatric therapy never dulled the power of the fantasies that ruled his life. In fact, his treatment would teach him how to con weak men like Bruce Hamill, to bend them to his will, and to make them become his hands, his eyes, his ears, when he killed again.

Woodcock arrived at Penetanguishene at 11:00 a.m. on April 20, 1957: Good Friday. A form filled out by the hospital's staff showed he had normal temperature, pulse and respiration. He was five feet, five and a half inches tall (he shrank somewhat over the years, and his poor posture made him look even shorter when he was in his fifties and sixties), weighed one hundred and five pounds, had hazel eyes and black hair. He was clean, with no noticeable vermin. He carried with him an electric razor and a nail file, which were turned over to the hospital bursar for safekeeping. In Woodcock's suitcase was a bathrobe, three Bibles, a suit, a pair of eyeglasses, a handkerchief, and some street clothes.

Less than a month after Woodcock arrived at Oak Ridge, he was taken back to Toronto. Finally, justice was about to be done for Ron Moffatt, the boy who had been jailed in the dreadful Guelph Reformatory for the murder of Wayne Mallette. A few days before the hearing, three men had come to see Woodcock: his lawyer, John Brooke; a Mr. Hartt, who was the lawyer for Moffatt; and a Metro police officer, all of whom wanted to be sure that Woodcock would testify to his guilt. There was some foot-dragging by Oak Ridge officials. Some of them believed that Woodcock might be confessing to a crime that he had read about in the newspapers.

For a week, Woodcock was in Toronto, staying at the old Queen Street asylum. At the end of a short hearing in one of Toronto's City

Hall courtrooms, Moffatt was finally set free. He had spent almost a year locked up for a murder he didn't commit, and for about half of that time the authorities knew that he was innocent.

Moffatt's mother told newspapers that her son had been through hell: drug treatments by doctors who believed he was lying about his innocence; a trial that ended in a miscarriage of justice; months locked up as a child murderer, at the bottom of the Guelph reform school pecking order.

After a hearing with lawyers for Ron Moffatt and Ontario prosecutors in the chambers of the Chief Justice of the Ontario Court of Appeal, Moffatt's conviction was quashed and a new trial ordered. The prosecutors realized they had the wrong suspect and Moffatt was freed three weeks later from the tough Guelph Reformatory west of Toronto. Judge Stewart, who made the final order, remarked briefly on the strange confession that had done so much to convict Moffatt:

"I have suggested to the police that in all cases where statements are being taken from juveniles, there should be present either the parents, or one of the parents, or some other disinterested person such as a minister, priest or teacher; if they are not available, at least some other person not connected with the police, and I would suggest that practice is advisable and if it were followed it would be unlikely to have a situation arise as did arise from this particular case.

"In the case of Peter Woodcock, he was a person declared to be of unsound mind, but on the evidence presented I have held that he was a competent witness. While there are some discrepancies in his statement, the evidence of Dr. Spence (the psychiatrist who examined Woodcock) is consistent with Woodcock's statement and is inconsistent with the confession of Ronald Moffatt. Consideration of the evidence as a whole leaves me with reasonable doubt, in fact, I must say, a substantial doubt as to the guilt of Ronald Moffatt. He is entitled to the benefit of that doubt and I therefore find him not guilty of the offence for which he has been charged."

The judge told Moffatt to stand up.

"I have found you not guilty of the charge laid against you, the charge to which you confessed to the police, and the evidence here you swore what you told the police that you committed this crime and gave a good many details in connection with it, and the story you said was untrue. All I have to say to you is this. You of course yourself know whether your statement was true or not. If it was not true then you have brought it upon yourself, all the trouble you have been in, in connection with this case, all the trouble given your parents, simply because you failed to tell the truth.

"I hope you will, at least, learn this from this trial, and you will never forget it, and whatever trouble you get into, and you may have some temporary advantage by telling something untrue, but it will always be to your advantage to tell the truth, and if you are in the wrong, take your punishment."

At the end of the hearing, Moffatt was given back to his sobbing parents. In 1957, that was as much as he or his family could hope for.

The Mallette family, confused and angry that a mentally-ill man's testimony had freed a boy who had confessed to Wayne's killing, went back to Seeley's Bay, swearing they would never again set foot in Toronto. "I wonder if they think Wayne committed the crime himself," John Mallette wrote to the Toronto police. "It looks very much that way. No one guilty."

\*\*\*

*Author's Note* - Going back over Woodcock's file, I saw lingering doubts among some of his therapists that Woodcock committed the Mallette murder. At times, Woodcock himself seemed unclear in his interviews with psychiatrists. He would sometimes act as though he didn't trust his memory and say that, since he worked Saturday nights at Casa Loma, he might not have been able to commit the crime. If that was so, then, perhaps, another killer might have gone free.

One day in the summer of 1996, when Krueger phoned me to chatter about something trivial, I decided to ask him if he killed Wayne. He was in a rather jovial mood, happier than he had been in several weeks. The hospital had issued an edict earlier in the summer that he quit telling jokes to other patients. That rule had been lifted.

So, did he kill Wayne Mallette?

"Oh, yes," he said.

Why did he bother helping Moffatt get out of jail?

"I was really angry that he was taking credit for something I did. It had bothered me since he was arrested, but I couldn't exactly come forward, could I?"

*** 

The summer and early fall of 1957 was a time of adjustment for Woodcock, and things didn't always go well. In the first spring, he was lonely and worried. No one who had committed murder, he was told, was ever released from Oak Ridge. Within weeks, though, he began feeling safe, despite his tiny size. Many of the other inmates, out of pity or lust, were kind. During the summer, he enjoyed the attention paid to him by four homosexual inmates who courted him and quarreled with each other. By October, however, he was depressed. He managed to get about a half meter of copper wire from an electrical cord, tie it into knots, and insert it deep into his penis. Attendants rushed to the screaming boy's room to find him lying on his cot, bleeding. They tried to pull the wire out, but it wouldn't budge. The next morning, when the Oak Ridge doctor arrived, he was given the task of removing the copper strip. Woodcock was given a "whiff of anesthesia," according to his medical report, and the doctor gave the wire a stiff pull. Woodcock spent the rest of the day in a cold bath.

Oak Ridge staff tried to cover up the self-mutilation. When Susan Maynard came to visit a few days later, she saw that Peter was unwell, but he told her that he had the flu. The institution's staff supported the lie, saying that a cold virus was wafting through Oak Ridge's wards.

Still, Susan Maynard worried. Just after Woodcock's first Christmas in Oak Ridge, she sent a plaintive letter to his psychiatrist. For the next ten years, there was a steady stream of correspondence, but by the late 1960s, it tapered off. Krueger doesn't know what happened to Susan Maynard and the rest of his foster family.

By the late fall of 1957, Woodcock's groin had healed. He broke out of his funk and became one of the busiest homosexuals on his ward, constantly in trouble for being in other men's cells.

Through the next couple of years, he developed the routine that he loved so very much: time with his friends, a few hours listening to radio, and working in the Oak Ridge library or kitchen. Woodcock always shied away from physical labor, and even in the library, where he could look through books all day, he was known as a slacker. He was more enthusiastic when he worked for the Oak Ridge newspaper, *The Quill*, and he liked to run the projector on movie nights. He liked to feel everything, like the buses, was running on schedule.

Ten years into his stay, after dozens of sexual relations, obsessions, run-ins with staff, and little acts of defiance and craziness, he was described in a report as a patient always looking for other inmates to have sex with, a braggart who expected other patients to be impressed by his crimes, but who, at the same time, told staff he felt remorse. His work in the typing and print shop was sloppy. He had full privileges, including the right to send and receive letters and have visitors, but few of either came for Woodcock. In the summer of 1967, he became obsessed with yet another patient, Steven Jones, who had spent time hanging around with the hippie crowd in Toronto's Yorkville counter-culture colony. The object of Woodcock's desire didn't share Peter's enthusiasm.

Woodcock followed the young man around "like a puppy," according to a social worker's report. Other inmates wanted the new patient, too. Woodcock reacted by sending them anonymous threatening letters. This was not a bright move by a small, nearsighted inmate without many friends. At least one fight broke out, which ended when Woodcock grabbed something sharp and cut a patient who was trying to restrain him.

The next year, his affections had settled on someone else. David Lesperance seems to have returned Woodcock's feelings, the two of them going so far as to agree to "Plan X," a suicide pact. When the guards found out about Plan X, Woodcock ended up shackled and locked in a strip safe-room, a cell with nothing in it but a cement slab to sleep on and an untearable denim blanket for warmth. Later, he was transferred to intensive therapy, and, by late summer, was back in his old cell.

Lesperance returned to Woodcock's ward a few months later. Desperate now, Woodcock took what little money he had and bought mod clothes. He let his hair grow long and tried to act like a hippie. It was no use: by Christmas, Lesperance had taken up with another inmate. Woodcock schemed to kill them both.

Soon, however, he got bored with that plan and found new things to do. There was too much going on around him. At the end of the 1960s, the counterculture had arrived at Penetanguishene. A crack had opened in the doors of Oak Ridge. Killers were starting to be released, and the place was becoming much more interesting for the inmates who were still inside. Inmates were fed a smorgasbord of hallucinogenic drugs. They didn't cure psychopaths, but they certainly broke up the boredom. Then, through the 1980s, cash-strapped governments began to look at ways of clearing out expensive psychiatric institutions. In 1992, Woodcock – now Krueger – had been locked up 35 years. It was time for him to go. His first day pass escort would be another killer, Bruce Hamill.

# KNIGHT OF THE PRAETORIAN GUARD

The Ottawa neighborhood of New Edinburgh is the kind of place where most Canadians would like to live. The shady streets are clean and safe. The Rideau River, fringed with parks and spanned by a lovely antique bridge, runs along the edge of the neighborhood. There's a strong sense of community, which shows itself in the support that New Edinburghers give to their churches and schools.

The Rideau Hall estate, home of the Governor General, marks the eastern boundary of the community. In the northwest corner, near the gates to Rideau Hall, is the Prime Minister's mansion at 24 Sussex Drive.

MacKay Street runs along the edge of the Rideau Hall estate, connecting to Sussex Drive less than a block from the Prime Minister's house. On the east side, the Governor General's residence is enclosed by a handsome wrought-iron fence. On the west side of the street, Bruce Hamill grew up in a little white-framed house, set back from the street. It's an ugly place. The house is pinched in between a much nicer home to the north and a duplex to the south. Most of the front yard is a driveway graveled in black mine slag.

The house backs on to a laneway. These little roads run behind most New Edinburgh houses. They give the local kids a safe place to learn how to ride their bikes and are easy shortcuts through the neighborhood. Kitty-corner to the back of the Hamill house is a ninety-year-old school. Bruce Hamill is one of its less-successful graduates, and he chose it to be the scene of his first murder.

Bruce Waldemar Charles Hamill was born on November 27, 1956. His mother was thirty-two, his father forty-seven. Fairly quickly, the Hamills realized Bruce had behavioral problems. He was born with a temporal lobe abnormality, which shows up on EEG and CAT scans. Through his childhood and teen years, Wally and Gertrude Hamill sheltered Bruce and tried to pretend that there was nothing seriously wrong with him. If he got into trouble, they blamed his friends. If he was in a fight, it was never his fault. They had found a psychiatrist for him, but the Hamill family did not believe he was dangerous. Sometimes, he had violent fits at home and lashed out at the family, but they told themselves his anger was just part of life for a young man who had trouble fitting in.

Bruce's emotional problems were just part of the strange dynamics of the Hamill household. Gertrude Hamill liked to believe that the world mistreated her entire family. She rose to the task of protecting her son from the outside world, even telling him not to take pills prescribed by his psychiatrist. Gertrude Hamill became a life-long victim, blaming the government, the city, her neighbors, and any other outsiders who crossed her, for her troubles. Her son saw himself as her protector.

As a teenager, Bruce's rages became more frequent. By Grade 10, he was buying street drugs from the dealers in downtown Ottawa. He had a few odd jobs and, when he turned eighteen, spent a summer in the militia. After he got home, Hamill became more violent. A few months after he left the army base at Petawawa, Hamill went to visit a homosexual friend. They smoked marijuana and drank until the gay man passed out. Hamill raised a knife over the man's exposed back, then ran the blade along his back, side and stomach. He wondered what it would feel like to plunge the blade in. This time, Hamill stopped himself.

Just after Christmas, he beat a twelve-year-old boy to a pulp because the youth said something that Hamill took to be an insult. And, two weeks before he finally did kill someone, Hamill had gone to Ottawa's Lisgar Collegiate at the end of a school day to stab a student who had insulted him three years before. For days, Hamill had worked himself into a rage thinking about what the boy had said to him. The youth couldn't remember Hamill, had no idea why the man chased him around the school yard with a knife, and was lucky to get away alive.

Hamill's rage finally focused on Betty Wentzlaff, a fifty-eight-year-old janitor. She and her husband George had lived next to the Hamills for twenty-one years and had gone out of their way to be friendly with them. The Wentzlaffs had no children, so they gave some of their time to the Hamills. Gertrude and

Wally had invited Betty and George to their 25th anniversary party and the families often visited each other. Things between the neighbors were fine until Gertrude Hamill decided that she wanted the Wentzlaff house for her daughter. In her mind, the Wentzlaffs had no choice but to sell. When they refused, Gertrude Hamill began building a hatred-filled fantasy world with Betty Wentzlaff at the centre. Bruce watched his mother become fixated on Betty. While she would only complain about Mrs. Wentzlaff, Bruce was willing to act.

On the night of February 28, 1977, Gertrude Hamill called Betty Wentzlaff to ask her, once again, to sell her house to Bruce's sister. During the phone call, Bruce's mother shouted at Wentzlaff. She screamed that the neighbor was being unreasonable, that she wasn't grateful for the friendship she had been shown by the Hamills.

Bruce's mother was crying when she hung up the phone. Bruce decided he would fix the problem. He left the house, saying he was going to see a movie. Walking the streets of the village, along the outer fence of the Governor

General's estate and back towards MacKay Street, Bruce became more enraged. He thought about his mother, who had stayed loyal to him through the bad months. In his mind, Mrs. Wentzlaff became the persecutor of his family. She had deliberately set out to ruin the Hamill family and make his mother unhappy. He decided Betty Wentzlaff had to die.

For four years, Wentzlaff had worked as a part-time cleaner at Crichton Street School, just behind her house. Hamill followed her to work at about 5 a.m. In the darkness, Betty saw him climbing the fence behind his house and running after her. She tried to get into a side door of the school to escape, but Hamill caught up to her. He stabbed Betty twenty-seven times before scurrying back to his home.

Betty Wentzlaff was found dead about 6:45 a.m. by school superintendent Jean-Guy Charette, just three feet from the back door of the school. He thought she had fallen and hit her head on the ice. Charette ran inside the school, called police and found a blanket to cover her. When the police arrived and rolled her over, Charette and the police officers could see Wentzlaff had been stabbed in the upper abdomen and chest. Hours later, Charette was still crying in his office when a reporter phoned him."She was like a mother to everyone. Even the school children called her Betty," he told a reporter.

Police were baffled by the Wentzlaff murder. She had no enemies that anyone knew of. The more they learned about Betty Wentzlaff, the angrier and more determined the investigators became.

"It's just senseless," one detective told a local reporter. "How could a guy like that sleep at night, knowing what he has done? He has got to be crazy. He stabbed an old woman like that so many times."

Police quickly ruled out robbery, since Wentzlaff still had a small amount of money in her pocket. There was also no sign of sexual assault. At first, they believed she may have surprised an intruder in the school, but there was very little evidence to go on. Ice covered the ground at the murder scene, so there were no footprints. In the end, it was legwork, knocking on doors, that led them to suspect Hamill.

On Thursday morning, two days after Wentzlaff's murder, while Wally and Gertrude were shopping at the local IGA, police arrested Bruce. Once they had him in handcuffs, they searched the house, finding the knife that had been used to kill Betty. When Bruce's parents arrived home from the store, Bruce had been taken away, but the search was still going on. The police drove Wally and Gertrude to the police station and let them sit with their son in an interrogation room.

"They've charged me with murder," Bruce told his mother. "And I did it."

\*\*\*

Reporters crowded into a press conference later Thursday to learn about Hamill. Staff Superintendent Tom Flanagan told them: "We've recovered a number of things and taken them into our possession."

"Are you still looking for the knife?" a reporter asked.

"No," Flanagan answered. "We are no longer looking for a weapon."

The police praised the people of New Edinburgh for the dozens of tips that investigators received but were coy about how they had narrowed the search to Bruce Hamill.

"We knocked on virtually every door," Flanagan told reporters. "The whole police force was involved. The lack of evidence and the viciousness of the attack on Mrs. Wentzlaff made it a tough murder that had to be worked on in a very tough way."

Gertrude Hamill was more forthcoming with Kit Collins, an Ottawa Citizen reporter who knocked on her door just after noon. Wally Hamill was sitting in the kitchen when Gertrude ushered Collins inside the gloomy home.

"I had a premonition something was wrong," Wally told Collins.

"I didn't," Gertrude said. "Bruce went to a movie Monday night, then went for a pizza on Rideau Street. When he got home, we sat in the living room and ate it while we watched the late show. And in the morning, I didn't hear anything. Bruce usually slept until noon when he wasn't working. I woke up about six, the first time, then I got up at eight. Bruce was already up and dressed. We had a half a grapefruit each. Bruce said he had trouble sleeping."

Gertrude said she had no suspicions until she came home from the IGA and found the police rummaging through her house.

"My head feels like it wants to blow, but if that's the way that he's got to get help, okay. But he was getting help in the first place."

That afternoon, the pews of St. Luke's Lutheran Church in New Edinburgh were filled with about a hundred mourners. George Wentzlaff sat with his wife's mother. Six of Betty's brothers and sisters were nearby. The rest of the mourners were teachers and students from Crichton Street School, where the flag still flew at half mast.

\*\*\*

In the fall of 1978, Hamill was taken to Oak Ridge for assessment. Dr. Russell Fleming interviewed Hamill several times and came to the conclusion that the killer was legally sane at the time he stabbed Betty Wentzlaff.

Hamill tried to come across as a tough city kid who wouldn't let someone push around his family.

"I believe that if you fight people, they leave you alone. Mrs. Wentzlaff was a low-class, stupid woman who thought she could just push us around," Hamill told Dr. Fleming.

"What did you think about on the night of the murder?" Dr. Fleming asked.

"I thought about killing her. I didn't think about anything else. Like, I didn't think that I would get caught or anything. Afterwards, I was scared like hell. I knew that I did it, but I couldn't realize that I'd done it. Does that make sense? I saw my whole life go in front of me, thinking about the future."

"Your future?" Fleming asked.

"Yes," Hamill replied.

He stared out the window of the Oak Ridge ward sunroom for a few minutes, not saying anything.

"I don't remember what she looked like, even."

Hamill's tough exterior was starting to wear thin. He wanted Dr. Fleming to know why he committed the crime, that he had flipped out dozens of times over the years.

"If something had been done for me, if the medication had been stronger, maybe it wouldn't have happened. I guess I have a bad temper. My emotions go nuts on me. I can't go to prison. I wouldn't last a second. People waste away there like in a warehouse. If they send me here, I would work really hard. I'd even let them do surgery. I don't want to go to prison," he said.

\*\*\*

Hamill's trial began Monday, January 9, in Ottawa's old courthouse. For a little more than a week, psychiatrists would argue over the young man's sanity.

Dr. Selwyn Smith, head of forensic psychiatry at the Royal Ottawa Hospital, the city's main psychiatric institution, testified Mrs. Wentzlaff's murder was premeditated but the reasons behind it were irrational. He explained how the family was dysfunctional, how Bruce's mother saw herself as a victim, and her son as a protector. Bruce's brain damage was described, and Dr. Smith said it was difficult to treat. Drugs and, perhaps, surgical therapy could be effective, he said.

Under cross-examination by Crown prosecutor Andrejz Berzins, Dr. Smith stood by his conclusions and testified Bruce belonged in a psychiatric institution.

"Couldn't a penitentiary offer Mr. Hamill adequate care?" Berzins asked.

"That's a pious hope," Dr. Smith answered.

Other psychiatrists testified that Hamill didn't understand the nature and consequences of his crime. Although Hamill knew killing Wentzlaff was wrong, "he didn't feel it was wrong," said Dr. Frank Chalke, a consulting psychiatrist at the Royal Ottawa Hospital. "Originally, I felt that he did know. He planned on doing it. He formed the intention to do it."

Dr. David Bulmer, a psychiatrist at the Royal Ottawa Hospital, testified that Hamill's strange behavior at the time of the murder was evidence that he was having an epileptic fit brought on by his brain damage. The night before the killing, Hamill took a "sick pathological step in thinking that the something that had to be done was that she should be shot down. It would not have occurred to him that there were other ways of dealing with the situation."

Yes, Dr. Bulmer admitted under cross examination by prosecutor Berzins, Hamill was aware that he was stabbing Mrs. Wentzlaff and that she was going to die, "but at the time, he did not know that what he was doing was wrong."

Afterwards, he realized the wrongness of his actions but felt they "were not part of himself. Something had happened to him he felt was beyond his control. While he's undergoing a discharge, Bruce doesn't have the ability to make any meaningful choices."

Berzins fought the insanity defense, accusing Dr. Bulmer of trying to absolve Hamill of his responsibility for Wentzlaff's death by blaming his diseased mind, but Dr. Bulmer argued forcefully that Hamill really did lose touch with reality when he had his fits.

The day after Dr. Bulmer testified, the eleven men and one woman on the jury retired for two hours before delivering their verdict that they found Hamill not guilty by reason of insanity.

He stayed at Oak Ridge from January 1978 until December 1980, then was transferred to Brockville. At that institution, he was given day passes and gradually prepared for release. In March 1983, Hamill was freed. Five years later, he was discharged from his Warrant of the Lieutenant-Governor, the court order issued after the insanity verdict.

Nine years after killing Betty Wentzlaff, Hamill had no criminal record. He would, according to institutional policy, make a fit escort for Krueger on his first citizen-supervised day pass.

Meanwhile, Krueger was getting escorted trips all over Ontario. He visited a railway museum. He went to see *Silence of the Lambs*. Psychiatrists in Belleville, where Krueger now lived in a psychiatric hospital, thought they were seeing real progress. He was ready, they believed, to be escorted into the community by one of his friends.

# INITIATION DAY

It was hot and muggy on Saturday, July 13, 1991, when Bruce Hamill, a physically and mentally twisted young man, rode the elevator down from his eighth floor apartment in suburban Ottawa and headed for a bus stop. A few minutes later, he was on his way to the capital's modern black steel and glass railway station. As the bus carried him closer to the train terminal, he could see the Peace Tower and the neo-Gothic Parliament Buildings rising above the office blocks of downtown Ottawa.

The House of Commons was a place where he had always wanted to work, but he couldn't get a security clearance. The RCMP and CSIS don't usually give those out to murderers. Instead, Hamill found a job at the county courthouse and a seniors' home, places where criminally insane killers met whatever criteria existed for security guards. The judges, lawyers and elderly people had no idea what was going on in the mind of the man who was paid to guard them. When they did learn more about Bruce Hamill, the people who had known him during his short career as a security guard would shudder with dread.

The Ottawa train station is not a busy place, so it didn't take Hamill, who was dressed in jeans and a t-shirt emblazoned with "ACE", very long to buy a ticket to Brockville. He had no baggage, except for a pipe wrench that he had wrapped in newspapers and put into two shopping bags. With a bit of a limp, he walked through the sliding doors of the station to the waiting train, a milk-run that stopped at the towns of the Ottawa Valley, the villages along the St. Lawrence River, and the small cities on the north shore of Lake Ontario before reaching Toronto five hours later. By late morning, he was travelling through the fields and woods of the flat land that lies between Ottawa and the St. Lawrence, through little Ottawa Valley towns like Smith's Falls.

He spent the hour of the trip trying to keep straight everything Mike had told him. Any deviation in the plan would cause it to fail. It wasn't just the outcome of the plot that was important. It was the ritual that mattered. If the timing was wrong, all of this would be for nothing.

As the train rolled through the countryside, which was still lush from the spring's heavy rains, Hamill thought about the problems he was having at home. His Philippines-born wife had begun to rebel over the visits to Brockville and, rightly, suspected Hamill was seeing a male lover. The Hamills had a baby girl that was adding strain to a marriage that was already explosive. The rage that had caused Hamill so much trouble in his life was building again. The fights were becoming more vicious. In recent weeks, Hamill had stopped talking at least to his wife. Now his inner thoughts were becoming more bizarre, and Mike was shaping and directing them.

\*\*\*

Hamill had been seeing Mike Krueger since 1989, but this visit was to be special: Krueger had been given his first day pass off the grounds of a psychiatric institution in thirty-five years. The Brockville hospital's staff thought Hamill and Krueger were going downtown to the Dairy Queen and for a walk along the St. Lawrence River. Then they were supposed to go to a Swiss Chalet. They would buy a pizza to take back to the hospital and spend the evening together. They, however, had other plans.

From the Brockville train station, Hamill limped down the main street until he found the town's Canadian Tire store. Its staff thought he looked weird as he lugged a heavy wad of newspaper through the air-conditioned aisles of the store. He stopped at the counter where guns and hunting knives were sold and spent more than an hour with a bored clerk, examining every blade, looking for just the right one. Then, taking much less time, he found a cheap hatchet and a sleeping bag.

"How will you be paying for that?" the store clerk asked as Hamill dropped his purchases on the counter with a clunk.

Hamill handed the woman a MasterCard. He stayed silent as she put it through the scanner. The card was valid. Hamill signed the paper that the clerk put in front of him while the woman stuffed everything into a big plastic bag.

"Can I put that in, too?" she asked, pointing at the newspaper-swaddled wrench.

"Sure," Hamill said.

The next stop was the town's drug store, where Hamill bought a pack of Nytol, a brand of over-the-counter sleeping pill. Then, after lugging his bag of weapons for about twenty minutes in the building heat, he stopped in a grove of trees, pulled everything out of the Canadian Tire bag and repacked the knife, hatchet and pipe wrench inside the sleeping bag. Ten minutes later, shortly after two in the afternoon, he was at the Brockville Psychiatric Hospital. He walked up to the receptionist at the front door, dropped the sleeping bag with its cargo of weapons on her counter, and told her he had arrived to escort Mike Krueger on a walk on the grounds.

A few minutes later, Krueger arrived from K-ward on the second floor of the hospital. He was dressed in a checkered shirt and a pair of shorts, his thinning hair cropped into a brush cut. Krueger was a short man with bandy legs and a pot belly. His face was forgettable, with small, piggy eyes, an average-sized nose, and poor bone structure. In proportion to his small body, his head seemed over-large. Krueger's hands were small, like those of a ten-year-old boy's. His skin was pale. That day, like most others, he probably had bad breath, and he squinted because of his lousy eyesight. He was also hard of hearing, although his deafness was rather selective.

Hamill signed Krueger out on what would be the first of two day passes. The Brockville institution has a large tract of land. Part of the grounds are lawns and gardens, but the acres of woods held more attractions for busy homosexuals like Krueger and Hamill, who had dubbed the forested part of the hospital lands "Procreation Park". In the weeks before this visit, they had picked out a special place in a sumac grove. Lugging the sleeping bag and its lethal contents, they headed for the shrubs. Within a few minutes, they had hidden the weapons along the trail through the bushes. On the way back to the hospital, they ran into another Brockville patient, Dennis Kerr. He was the person they were looking for.

Dennis was a skinny young man, somewhat younger-looking than his twenty-seven years, who was something of a jailhouse lawyer and a musician of moderate skill. Dennis believed Krueger had inherited a lot of money, and Kerr was supposed to borrow five hundred dollars to buy a set of used drums from a music store in Kingston. Krueger had spelled out exactly what the payments were to be, the rate of interest, and the collateral.

Kerr didn't know Krueger saw him as a "roaring street punk", a little thug who was better off dead. From Kerr's point of view, Krueger was just another horny old kiddy diddler on the hunt for men who looked like boys. Most of the other patients at Brockville felt the same way about Krueger. He was far down on the institution's social scale.

Kerr was introduced by Krueger to Hamill.

"Mr. Kerr, I'd like you to meet my good friend Bruce Hamill. Bruce, this is Dennis. In an hour, we'll be back with the money for you, Dennis. I just have to go back to my room to get it," Krueger said.

Kerr began to walk away.

Turning to Hamill, Krueger said in a stage whisper, "Dennis needs some money to buy a set of drums. We'll just give it to him, then we'll go into town."

Hamill flushed and Krueger chortled. They hurried back into the hospital, filled out the papers for the second escorted pass, this time lasting three hours. Hamill folded Krueger's day pass slip and stuck it in his pocket. Instead of heading into the town, they made their way to sumac grove, knowing that Kerr would soon be there to meet them.

Kerr arrived on time, not knowing that the bushes around him were salted with weapons. Hamill stood among the trees, but Krueger lay hidden in the bushes. As Kerr opened his mouth to ask where Krueger and the money was, he heard a slight yelp. Krueger, reaching for the pipe wrench, had sliced his finger on a pull tab from a pop can. Undeterred, Krueger raised the wrench and slammed it down on Kerr's head. Kerr turned to Krueger, cried out, "What did you do that for?" and slumped down, dying.

"I could barely lift the thing, let alone swing it," Krueger said, two years later. "I did manage to do it, and I got Dennis in the head. I hit him again, after he asked his little profound question, this time from the front, and he fell down, but not without a struggle. He struggled nearly the whole time. He seemed to be afraid to die."

Hamill and Krueger fished the knife and the hatchet out of their hiding spots and began stabbing and hacking at Kerr. The attack was part murder, part dissection. The killers sexually assaulted and mutilated Kerr. Krueger poked at the body, got close to hear the death rattle, and looked carefully at the vicious wounds that he and Hamill had inflicted.

"I wanted to see if Dennis had a death rattle. They really do exist. I sat next to his body for about an hour. When he died, I heard a sound like a deep snore that came from the middle of his body. That was the death rattle. Then I saw something like a mist that came from his mouth and went up towards the sky. I know it was his spirit."

Meanwhile, Hamill began his ritual. He and Krueger, both drenched in blood, sodomised Kerr's dead body, then began to chant. When Hamill was finished, he took the pills in the Nytol pack, walked a few paces from the corpse, and lay down in the sleeping bag. Within minutes, he was asleep. Krueger kept vigil over Kerr, still poking and peering at the body. When Hamill was finally out cold, Krueger walked up to him, pulled the sleeping bag down to look at Hamill's nude body, then began running the blade of the knife over Hamill's chest, down his stomach, and gently over the sleeping man's testicles. Krueger thought for a moment as he caressed Hamill's body with the knife. He was tired. This was enough.

Krueger used a pair of binoculars and a white cane to find his way to an Ontario Provincial Police station about five kilometers from the murder site. He walked up to the front counter and asked to speak with the officer in charge.

Very calmly, he spoke to Sergeant Terry Bowerman.

"I want to turn myself in. I've committed a horrible crime and I deserve to spend the rest of my life in a penitentiary," he told Bowerman.

"What have you done?" Bowerman asked Krueger. Bowerman looked over the counter at Krueger's bloody clothes.

"I killed someone. I didn't do it alone. There's another person involved. He's still there. He's a very dangerous man."

Bowerman called in Detective Sergeant Dave Bishop, a homicide expert. Bishop and two Brockville city police constables took Krueger back to the grounds of the psychiatric hospital. With Krueger squinting to see the path to the sumac grove, they set out to find Kerr's body. It was dark and raining when they arrived. Biting insects tormented the searchers. When they approached the hospital's power house, in an area of dense bush, Krueger told them they were near the scene. Soon, they found Hamill naked, thrashing around in the trees, tormented by bugs.

"Are you here to take me?" Hamill screamed. "I'm ready. I've done everything you want. Where do I go? Is your vehicle here?" he asked.

The police ordered Hamill to lie down. Instead, he ran toward Krueger and the four officers. Crazy from the drugs, confused and covered with bug bites, Hamill flew into a psychotic rage. For several minutes, he fought with the police before they were able to handcuff him and put him in a cruiser. Krueger took the two detectives down the trail to Kerr's body. They found Kerr about 200 meters from where they had tackled Hamill.

No police officer is so hardened that he could see something like the Kerr crime scene without being sick. The body was gutted. Kerr's head had been nearly severed from his torso. The little enclave in the sumacs was sticky with the young man's blood.

"It's such a shame," Krueger said. "Such a tragedy".

The police called for help from other detachments and radioed for an ambulance. Bowerman and another officer took Krueger back to the station. It took several hours for the police to take a couple of bizarre statements from Krueger and Hamill.

Hamill, still psychotic, was taken straight to the protective custody unit of the Brockville jail. Krueger stayed and talked with the police, spinning a tale that horrified the officers working the evening shift. Later, at a local hospital, Krueger got stitches for his cut hand, but he didn't take a shower until he was finally taken to the Brockville jail. During his time in the city police lockup, he masturbated in full view of the police. He kept doing it at the hospital, and through the night at the county jail. In all, police later recounted that Krueger masturbated at least six times in the first ten hours that he was in custody. Finally, he went to sleep, to be awakened a few hours later by a smell that he cherishes, and that he had missed for so long.

"Comes the morning, I wake up, and they're serving bacon and eggs because it's Sunday. I haven't had bacon and eggs in something like five years. And I thought to myself, 'fancy this, all I had to do to get bacon and eggs was commit murder. You literally have to kill somebody if you want a good breakfast in this system'." And, as he wolfed down his greasy fried eggs, his bacon and coffee, those last words of Kerr's kept going through his mind, stimulating him again and again.

"What did you do that for?"

The answer lay far away, long before Kerr was even born, in the mind of a very strange boy who prowled the streets of Toronto on a marvelous red three-speed bike. The boy who rode it back in the 1950s, like the dumpy little man, only killed on Saturdays.

# THE LAST ACT

On March 5, 2010, Krueger was found dead in his cell in Oak Ridge. It was his 71st birthday. One more time, he made the front page of the *Toronto Star* as "the serial killer they couldn't cure." Very soon afterwards, Oak Ridge itself was gone, torn down and replaced by a new, more humane institution.

In the end, nothing was Krueger's fault.

Not the killings of the kids. Wayne Mallette, Gary Morris and Carole Voyce died in a series of "accidents," which were "tragedies" for all the people involved. And accidents can happen to anyone. Dennis Kerr was killed at the Brockville Psychiatric Hospital in 1992 in an act of mercy, not an act of rage and lust. And, after all of those killings, the courts had said Peter Woodcock, or David Michael Krueger, was not guilty by reason of insanity. Not guilty. Didn't do it. Accident. Incident. Tragedy. Never a crime committed by this strange little man on people who deserved no harm.

And with Bruce Hamill, it's the same. Poor Mrs. Wentzlaff was stabbed to death near the door of a school in Ottawa in what the principal who knew better called an "accident." It happened because Hamill had an organic brain disease, not because Hamill was a miserable young man with a taste for heavy drugs and a weird attachment to his mother. When he helped Mike Krueger kill Dennis Kerr, it was that brain disease at work again. Not guilty by reason of insanity. Not culpable. Fished in.

That's the way Krueger told it. Could have happened to you or me or anyone who had been dealt a bad hand by fate. But he was not like you and me. Something awful lived inside that man. As I left Oak Ridge visitors' centre one day, Krueger looked at a Childfind poster of missing kids. He smiles, points, and says, "that one, that one, and that one."

Peter Woodcock was guilty.

## About Crimes Canada: True Crimes That Shocked the Nation

This is a multi-volume twenty-four book collection, (one per month, each approximately 100 to 180 pages) project by crime historian Dr. Peter Vronsky and true crime author and publisher RJ Parker, depicting some of Canada's most notorious criminals.

Crimes Canada: True Crimes that Shocked the Nation will feature a series of Canadian true crime short-read books published by *VP Publications* (Vronsky & Parker), an imprint of *RJ Parker Publishing, Inc.*, one of North America's leading publishers of true crime.

Peter Vronsky is the bestselling author of *Serial Killers: The Method and Madness of Monsters* and *Female Serial Killers: How and Why Women Become Monsters* while RJ Parker is not only a successful publisher but also the author of 18 books, including *Serial Killers Abridged: An Encyclopedia of 100 Serial Killers*, *Parents Who Killed Their Children: Filicide*, and

*Serial Killer Groupies*. Both are Canadians and have teamed up to share shocking Canadian true crime cases not only with fellow Canadian readers but with Americans and world readers as well, who will be shocked and horrified by just how evil and sick "nice" Canadians can be when they go bad.

Finally, we invite fellow Canadians, aspiring or established authors, to submit proposals or manuscripts to *VP Publications* at *Editors@CrimesCanada.com*.

VP Publications is a new frontier traditional publisher, offering their published authors a generous royalty agreement payable within three months of publishing and aggressive online marketing support. Unlike many so-called "publishers" that are nothing but vanity presses in disguise, VP Publications does not charge authors in advance for submitting their proposal or manuscripts, nor do we charge authors if we choose to publish their works. We pay you, and pay well.

## Acknowledgments

*Thank you to my editor, proof-readers, and cover artist for your support:*

### - - Mark Bourrie

Aeternum Designs (book cover), Bettye McKee (editor), Dr. Peter Vronsky (editor), RJ Parker Publishing, VP Publications, Lorrie Suzanne Phillippe, Marlene Fabregas, Darlene Horn, Ron Steed, Katherine McCarthy, Robyn MacEachern, Kim Jackson, Lee Knieper Husemann, Kathi Garcia, Vicky Matson-Carruth, Cynthia Wood, Amanda Hutchins, Linda Bergeron

# Books in the Crimes Canada Collection

An exciting 24-volume series collection, edited by crime historian Dr. Peter Vronsky and true crime author and publisher RJ Parker.

VOLUMES:

(URL LINK ON NEXT PAGE)

1. Robert Pickton: The Pig Farmer Killer by C.L. Swinney
2. Marc Lepine: The Montreal Massacre by RJ Parker

3. Paul Bernardo and Karla Homolka by Peter Vronsky

4. Shirley Turner: Doctor, Stalker, Murderer by Kelly Banaski

5. Canadian Psycho: Luka Magnotta by Cara Lee Carter

6. The Country Boy Killer: Cody Legebokoff by JT Hunter

7. The Killer Handyman by C.L. Swinney

8. Hell's Angels Biker Wars by RJ Parker

9. The Dark Strangler by Michael Newton

10. The Alcohol Murders by Harriet Fox

View these and future books in this collection at:

***rjpp.ca/CC-CRIMES-CANADA-BOOKS***

## ABOUT THE AUTHOR

Mark Bourrie, PhD (History) has been a member of the Parliamentary Press Gallery since 1994. He previously taught media history and journalism at Concordia University. Mark is the author of eleven books. The most recent, *Kill the Messenger: Stephen Harper's Assault on Your Right to Know*, was placed on the

Globe and Mail list of top 100 books of 2015. *The Fog of War: Censorship of Canada's Media in The Second World War* reached No. 6 on Maclean's magazine's bestseller list in 2011, and *Fighting Words: Canada's Best War Reporting*, was published last fall. Bourrie has won several major media awards, including a National Magazine Award, and has been nominated for several others. His journalism has appeared in the Globe and Mail, the Toronto Star, the National Post, Montreal Gazette, Ottawa Citizen, and most of the country's major newspapers and several magazines including Toronto Life and Ottawa magazine. He is also a consultant on propaganda and censorship at the Canadian Forces Public Affairs School.

*"If you enjoyed reading this book, please take a moment to leave a brief review on Amazon, Goodreads and any other market. Your feedback is very important to the author and publisher."*

**Thank you,**

**Mark Bourrie**

RJ Parker / Peter Vronsky (VP Publications)

## CONTACT INFORMATION

**Twitter**

*https://twitter.com/markbourrie*

**Amazon's Author Page**

*http://www.amazon.com/Mark-Bourrie/e/B001HMPSIY*

**Email**

*Mbourrie@Yahoo.com*

**Facebook**

*https://www.facebook.com/mark.bourrie.1*

Printed in Great Britain
by Amazon.co.uk, Ltd.,
Marston Gate.